Are You on the Right Bus?

Are You on the Right Bus?
Navigating Change on the Road to Success
...and lessons learned at every stop

Angela M. Burgess

All Rights Reserved. No portion of this book may be reproduced, stored in a retrieval system, or transmitted in any form or by any means -- electronic, mechanical, photocopy, recording, scanning, or other -- except for brief quotations in critical reviews or articles without the prior permission of the author.

Published by Game Changer Publishing

Cover Photography by Chris Gillet
Illustrations by Ashlyn Dailey

Paperback ISBN: 978-1-961189-77-5
Hardcover ISBN: 978-1-961189-78-2
Digital: ISBN: 978-1-961189-80-5

www.GameChangerPublishing.com

DEDICATION

For my loving husband. Thank you for believing in me and making me laugh when I take it all too seriously. For my dear friends who have supported me and this project with enthusiasm and constructive feedback: Alena, Alissa, Natasha, and Sarah - thank you for putting in the time to make this book the best it can be. To everyone who graciously accepted the invitation to join my book launch team, thank you for your excitement and support. Last, but certainly not least, a special thanks to my parents for always allowing me the space to be me, even when I am difficult to understand; for encouraging me to pursue my dreams, even when my dreams may seem foreign or unrelatable; and for loving me unconditionally throughout my journey.

Read This First

If you're a nonprofit leader looking to partner with someone who has a long track record of growing sustainable businesses in both the for profit and nonprofit sectors, or an organization or company looking for a keynote speaker at your next event who will inspire and motivate your audience to action, schedule a consultation with Broad Oaks Consulting!

Scan this Code:

Oh, and just so you know, simply by purchasing this book, you've changed someone else's life. 10% of all book proceeds are donated to charities transforming communities. Thanks for being awesome!

Are You on the Right Bus?

Navigating Change on the Road to Success

...and lessons learned at every stop

Angela M. Burgess

www.GameChangerPublishing.com

Table of Contents

Foreword 1

Preface 5

Introduction 7

Chapter 1 – Why Are We Talking About Buses? 11

Chapter 2 – We Don't Always Have a Choice in Travel 19

Chapter 3 – This Is as Far as This Bus Goes 31

Chapter 4 – Chartering Your Own Bus 39

Chapter 5 – Let Me On! 49

Chapter 6 – Traveling Alone 67

Chapter 7 – The Rowdy Bus 79

Chapter 8 – New Passengers 89

Chapter 9 – There is More than One Way to Travel 99

Chapter 10 – You Haven't Lived Until You've Been Escorted off the Bus 115

Chapter 11 – The New Bus Company 129

Chapter 12 – Starting My Own Bus Line 149

Chapter 13 – Driving the Bus 163

Chapter 14 – When the Bus Crashes 183

Chapter 15 – Scaling the Bus Line 195

Afterward 205

Works Cited in this Book 209

Foreword

Dear fellow traveler:

Whether you are still in school or well into your career, I have good news: You are on the right bus, at least when it comes to picking up this book.

If you've been wondering what you should do when you "grow up," this book won't give you *the* answer, but it will help you find *your* answer.

If you've been wondering if you're going down the right path in life, this book won't just help you arrive at a "yes" or a "no"; it will also help you figure out what to do about it.

If you've been helping someone else wrestle with these questions, whether as a mentor, manager, teacher, friend, or loved one, this book won't just help you figure out what to say; it will also help you grasp how your actions—and how, in turn, you—will be remembered decades from today.

Angela the 7th grader once believed that she was a 'B' student because that was what she was told growing up at home. Then, one day, a certain teacher looked at Angela in the eye and said: "You're an 'A' student performing at a 'B' level."

Are *you* an 'A' "student" performing at a 'B' level?

Now, look around. How many people that the universe has assigned to your care are also 'A' "students" performing at a 'B' level?

In the pages to come, Angela—former-self-proclaimed-B-student-in-an-A-student's-body, will walk you through how to find your place in the world—and how to build a career and life helping others find their place also.

The universe could not have found a better messenger for this important message. As Angela will share in Chapter Thirteen ("Driving the Bus"), Angela and I met when RaiseUp Families, the nonprofit that Angela leads as Executive Director, incorporated my book, *The Unspoken Rules*, into its program to help families climb out of poverty. As the son of a working-class single mother who became a first-generation college student at Harvard, I never had a parent or mentor whispering in my ear growing up to show me how to navigate college applications, internships, or the world of white-collar work.

I wrote *The Unspoken Rules* to level the playing field—and to empower talent from humble beginnings and underrepresented backgrounds to navigate the professional world with confidence. Little did I know that Angela's "bus" and mine would meet on this highway of life. And I'm so glad ours did.

When I traveled to Houston to speak at RaiseUp Families' annual Graduation Celebration in April of 2023, I saw Angela and the souls she's impacted: a community of 250 who came together to celebrate 31 families transformed for the better. I met the single mother of an autistic boy who got promoted twice and more than doubled her salary—all in nine months. I also met an overnight security guard who successfully secured a corporate job with stable pay and benefits, along with countless other families who escaped eviction, homelessness, and bankruptcy. Moreover, I met the case management, professional staff, and donor community that made it all happen—all under Angela's leadership.

Angela shares in Chapter Seven ("The Rowdy Bus"): "Leadership consists of thousands of little things that make a big difference." If this is true, then, through knowing Angela, I found a thousand reasons why her story is one that is worth reading.

I can still remember the afternoon Angela drove me to the airport after the Graduation Celebration. As I got out of the car, I turned around and asked, "So, when are you going to write a book? I'd totally read it!"

"Actually, I'm writing one," Angela smiled. "Could you write the foreword?" I smiled back. And teared up.

And, after reading this book, I teared up again.

Welcome to the bus,

— Gorick Ng
Wall Street Journal Bestselling Author,
The Unspoken Rules: Secrets to Starting Your Career Off Right

Preface

I've always been envious of people who just knew what they wanted to be. From the time she was a little girl, my friend Cheryl knew she wanted to be a veterinarian like her dad. Alissa always knew she wanted to be an educator like her parents. José Altuve knew he wanted to be a baseball player, and Tiger Woods knew he was destined to be a golfer.

How grand life must be to know exactly what you want to be when you grow up, and to be able to follow a path others have trod before you, the way already paved!

After decades of building and leading teams, I've concluded that most of us are not, in fact, that lucky. Regardless of race, religion, or socioeconomic background, most of us have no idea what we want to be when we grow up because we have no idea what we can be.

If you had asked me as a kid growing up in Iowa what I wanted to be, I probably would have said something like, "I want to help people and make a difference." It turns out you cannot major in "helping people" or "making a difference" in college. If you look at my career on paper, you might think I lack direction, stick-to-it-iveness, or commitment. Maybe you look at my resume and think that I fail a lot and, therefore, start over a lot.

The opposite is actually true. The truth about my CV is that at a young age, I embraced what I was passionate about and good at, and I poured my heart and soul into committing to excellence in those areas. I was fortunate to cross paths with people who took the time to offer advice, observations, and counsel, and I was brave enough to listen. Every experience I've had and position I've held has allowed me to learn and grow and has been a stop on my road to success.

– Angela

Introduction

Every morning, you wake up, get ready for work, hop on the bus, and sit in your regular window seat, third row from the front. Life has become so repetitive that you are now on autopilot, unaware that deep down you feel defeated and lost. As you stare out the window, the bus suddenly hits a BUMP, jerking you back to reality. Shocked, you look around and realize... is this really the seat you want to be sitting in? Is this bus going to the destination you're trying to get to? Heck, are you even on the right bus?

It feels like something is missing in your life. As a talented and hardworking individual, you want to align your skills and passions with a thriving career. But how do you do that? Finding the confidence to make big changes is scary, but you have something extraordinary to contribute to the world! It is time to break free from your comfort zone and embark on a transformative journey that will unlock your true potential as a leader.

In June 2021, I was invited to speak to a group of high school sophomores, juniors, and seniors who had been accepted to a development program in Houston, Texas, called Atlas Scholars which offers mentorship, scholarships, and exposure to performance-based professional environments. Every week, they host a guest speaker and I was there to speak about entrepreneurship.

Imagine my surprise when, at the conclusion of my presentation, among the first questions I received was, "What do you do if your parents are encouraging you to pursue something that offers stability rather than pursuing your passions and dreams?"

In that moment, I realized my path to entrepreneurship held far more value than my arrival. If my story could prevent even one person from pursuing a stable, unfulfilling life, and inspire them to embrace all that makes them unique and connect their passion with purpose, then it was worth putting on paper.

This book is intended to open your eyes to the fact that life isn't just one long ride. It's a series of arrivals, departures, travel companions, starts, and stops. The key is being able to recognize if you are in the right seat on the right bus, finding the humility to change seats (or give yours up for someone else) when necessary, and having the courage to change buses altogether when it turns out you're not on the right bus at all.

From the day my parents brought me home from the hospital, I was a rule follower. I rarely cried and slept through the night practically from the first day I arrived home. I had a healthy respect for authority and was, by all accounts, a happy and content child - until the 8th grade.

Around age 13, I began having dreams of greatness. At thirteen, "greatness" meant being the 1st chair flutist in band and getting straight A's. As a young person, I did not give a lot of consideration to how my faith formed my everyday life. I was raised in the Presbyterian Church as was a faithful disciple of Christ, but my faith life and my everyday life were very separate. One had absolutely nothing to do with the other.

As I got older, "greatness" meant embracing who I was and harnessing the gifts God gave me to make a difference in the world. As you'll read in the chapters ahead, my road to success is paved in the pursuit of inspiring transformative change in our world by helping others achieve goals and dreams they either didn't know they had or believed to be beyond reach. My ability to do this stems from my God-given gifts of leadership and service (which show up time and again in every personality test I take—religious or secular). However, my courage to do this work stems from knowing what bus I'm on and the ease with which I've come to accept when it's time to change seats, ask people to get off my bus, welcome new passengers on, or pull the cord and change buses at the next stop.

It is my sincere hope that you find inspiration, perspective, and courage in these pages. Thank you for sharing in my story and allowing me into your world for a moment in time.

"To lead yourself, use your head; to lead others, use your heart."

-John Maxwell

CHAPTER ONE

Why Are We Talking About Buses?

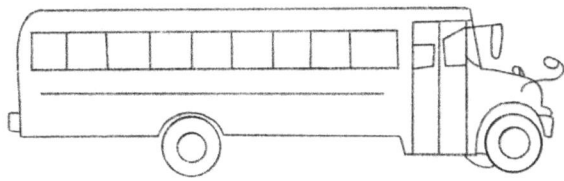

Early in my career, I remember reading about the concept of being in the right seat on the bus. It is a thought I have returned to time and again and shared with others, so much so that family, friends, and colleagues regularly ask me, "Hey, when are you going to write that book about the bus?"

As I embarked on this book-writing journey, I honestly couldn't remember who wrote about the bus or came up with the concept. It was Jim Collins in his 2001 book, *Good to Great*. (My sincere apologies to Mr. Collins for my memory lapse. It is still a "must-read" for any leader or aspiring leader.)

Good to Great encompasses what leaders need to do in order to see their teams excel. The bus concept posits that achieving your goal or reaching your destination is not necessarily about steering your people in the right direction, but about getting the right group of people moving in a **forward** direction **together** and getting the wrong people off the bus.

What I love about the bus concept is that it first opens your eyes to the fact that you're in a moving vehicle. We are constantly moving forward. And like any forward-moving vehicle (buses included), we're going to need to stop. Buses are unique because they tend to make frequent stops. From time to time, people will pull the cord because they want to get off. New people will get on the bus. Sometimes people get rowdy, and other times people may even be escorted off the bus. Maybe *you're* the one who needs to be escorted off.

Adapting this concept to your work life allows you to learn one very critical and valuable lesson: you are never stuck. You are never trapped. While you are in a vehicle that is in constant forward motion, there are myriad opportunities to stop, reassess, get off, and make a different choice.

The key is being able to recognize the bus you are on and evaluate if you are surrounded by the right people who can help you arrive at your desired destination. Sometimes we find ourselves on a bus surrounded by great people, but it turns out they are headed somewhere we really do not want to go. This is what I realized after about a year into my first job after college. I was surrounded by many great people, but I truly had no interest in arriving at their final destination. Sure, it was stable work, and there was a growth path in sales, but imagining myself in any senior position there did not fill me with joy. As I pictured my future self, she made a living, but what about a life worth living?

As you think about your life and career, ask yourself: are you headed to your target, or desired destination, or are you just along for the ride?

You will never arrive at your desired destination with the wrong passengers. "Wrong" doesn't necessarily mean "bad." It may simply be that your fellow passengers are headed in a direction you have no intention of visiting. Perhaps you change your mind halfway through the ride and decide you actually want to go somewhere else. This exercise is about finding like-minded people that are headed in the same general direction as you to help you navigate your way to scalable success—whatever that means to you. When everyone is clear and in alignment with the destination, and each passenger is intrinsically motivated to arrive, the path—or route—will take care of itself.

As my life progressed, this analogy grew way beyond my professional world. I realize now that life is just a series of buses that we hop on and off. Some of us are more comfortable with frequent changes than others. The reality is that we change buses in small ways a thousand times a day as we strive to make forward progress in the various aspects of our lives.

You're on one bus when you're taking your kids to school. You stop and transfer to another bus when you're headed into your workplace; you transfer again when you head to the gym or volunteer work when you leave the office.

We are all okay with these small transfers. We adjust to scheduling changes and delays, we change seats, and we sometimes change routes entirely with relative ease. But when it comes to the long journey—the one that will ultimately define our life and the mark we leave behind on the world—our tendency is to stay in a comfort zone, even if that means relentlessly pursuing a destination we have no real interest in visiting. We can visit our desired destinations once we have made our millions and have more free time, right?

Stop for a moment and think about the different parts of your life in which you are trying to affect a future outcome. For parents, it may be creating an environment in which your children can grow, thrive, and make memories. For professionals, it may be getting that dream job or, better yet, discovering your dream job and finding a way to make it work financially. For activists, it may be building an organization or movement that creates greater equity or social justice in the world. Now imagine that each of those areas is its own bus. Who is on each bus? Do they share your same sense of clarity and alignment? If you could add any passenger to a bus to help guide it to your desired destination, who would it be? Who doesn't belong on the bus? And if no one on the bus sees the destination as clearly as you do, is the problem the passengers, or are you on the wrong bus?

Accepting when it is time to make a change is the most difficult part. As humans, we are mostly change-averse. We would rather live in insanity—doing the same things over and over again, expecting different results—than admit that what we are doing or the role we are filling is not moving us toward our desired outcomes. Change is hard. Change makes us feel defeated. Change makes us think that we have been doing something wrong all this time. Change makes us feel weak because we're now trying something we've never done before, and we probably won't be good at it right away. So, it's better to do the same thing we're good at, over and over again, rather than make a change and potentially experience defeat.

We all consciously know none of this is true. We know that change is a natural part of life, and those who embrace it grow while those who do not slowly die, metaphorically. Two of the largest obstacles to change are ego and pride. Moving out of our own way is the toughest battle most of us will face. Giving up our seat for someone else, stepping down when it's time for someone else to step up, and gracefully exiting when we have added all the value we can, are what we should all strive for. Know when to pull the cord and patiently wait for the next stop.

Equally important is knowing when to harness your inner Keanu Reeves or Sandra Bullock, like in the movie *Speed*. Make no mistake, there are times when we feel as though we're being held captive on a bus moving at 70 miles per hour, the bus is on fire, there's someone trying to kill us, and there's no clear way to make a safe exit. There is little grace or patience to be found on that bus trip, and your only recourse may be hurling yourself to the front of the bus, yanking the bus driver out of his seat, slamming on the brakes, swinging open the doors while the bus is still moving, then launching yourself out the doors like a stunt man. It happens. Your bus may get hijacked. That's what I call a toxic environment.

So, why are we talking about buses? Because they are an outstanding metaphor for the close-knit circles of people we create around us—in all aspects of our lives—to help drive us forward in our quest to overcome insurmountable odds on our own personal road to success.

Lessons Learned:

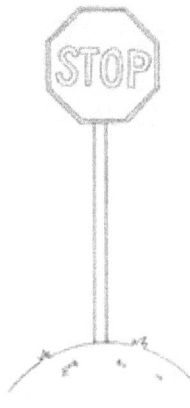

1. Life is not one, long journey. It is a series of starts and stops, with opportunities to make different choices along the way.

2. We are the single biggest obstacle to change in our lives.

3. What bus are you on, and are you surrounded by the people who will help you reach your desired destination?

CHAPTER TWO

We Don't Always Have a Choice in Travel

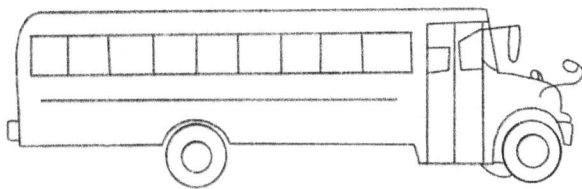

Despite what flight attendants may tell you upon landing, "We know you have a choice in travel, and we thank you for choosing [fill in the airline]," the truth is that we do not, in fact, always have a choice in travel. In most developed nations, the only bus available throughout formative years is the school bus. In the book *Dark Horse: Achieving Success through the Pursuit of Fulfillment*, authors Todd Rose and Ogi Ogas dive into the history of educational standardization and its impact on perceptions, beliefs, lives, and culture. As I processed their message, what I found fascinating about standardized education is that for many people—and for me, in particular—it is the passengers on the school bus that have the single largest impact on our journey and, ultimately, our destination.

Teachers decide who we spend time with through assigned seating, the groups to which we are assigned, and the opportunities offered to advance our education. Standardized testing determines our aptitude and next academic opportunities. As a result, I struggled in school as a youngster.

Kindergarten got off to a rocky start for me socially when my kindergarten teacher assigned me friendships with two of the least-liked kids in school. While I have no recollection of it, my mom has shared with me on numerous occasions that I used to come home in tears, begging her not to make me go back. We all know kids can be mean, and while my teacher was well-intentioned, trying to help two kids who did not fit in find kindness and compassion in me, what she did not see was that the outcome was all three of us being ostracized and cast out by the other students.

By first grade, I already disliked school, and I decided that I didn't want to do any of the work. Mrs. Hemingway had a reward system where, when we finished the worksheet we were supposed to be working on in math, reading, or writing, we could get a "fun" worksheet from the front of the classroom to work on while our classmates completed their assignments. I quickly realized I did not need to do the actual work. As soon as the assignment was handed out, I shoved it in my desk, walked to the front of the room, got a "fun" worksheet, and proceeded to color for the rest of the hour.

This went on for months until my desk would no longer close. Mrs. Hemingway finally called my parents to a special parent/teacher meeting and said, "Angie's bright, but she is not doing any of the work in this class. She's falling behind." My parents came home and asked me if what Mrs. Hemingway had said was true. "I don't want to do the work," I replied. "I'd rather just do the fun worksheets."

Lesson one: Life isn't about just having fun. You have to do the work. Just like at home, where you have to do your chores before you can watch TV, at school, you have to do the work before you can do the fun worksheets. It took me about a month to get through the backlog of assignments. I did not get to watch TV after school or go out and play until I was all caught up on assignments, and my desk would once again close. On a positive note, I really understood how this whole "do the work, get rewarded" concept went.

I grew up in a middle-class family in Iowa. My parents are hardworking folks; both worked full-time, and we had a quiet, comfortable life. As a kid, it always seemed like my older brother, Chris, got most of the attention most of the time, which was annoying. Maybe it's just because I'm his little sister, but it always seemed to me he could do anything. He was highly intelligent. The same assignments that it took me a month to get through, my brother could do in 10 minutes. When he was in the sixth grade, he decided that he wanted to try out for band. The only problem was band auditions were the next day, and Chris did not play an instrument. The band director lent him a saxophone, and in one night, he learned all of the major and minor scales. I had played the piano for three years at that point and still couldn't play all the major and minor scales from memory.

It was mind-numbingly frustrating. He was that kid who never had to study and could make good grades, was always goofing off, and had a ton of friends. Everything seemed so easy for him. For me, on the other hand, everything was hard work. Why do you think I was putting aside the work assignments and going straight to the fun worksheets? Everything required effort for me. I never felt good about myself or my abilities. I lacked confidence.

I wanted, more than anything, to be smart. The "popularity bus" had passed me by in kindergarten, and I desperately wanted to be picked up by the smart bus. My parents had this collection of books downstairs, including a book on shorthand. My maternal grandmother knew how to take shorthand, and I thought surely this would be my gift. I would show up to the 2nd grade, able to take shorthand, and would be able to record everything the teacher said. Nothing could stop me then! But when I opened up that shorthand book, I had no idea what it was saying. It was like I was reading a completely foreign language.

Rather than asking my grandma for help, I just closed the book and decided that I must not be very smart after all. That title was reserved for Chris. He was smart; I was a hard worker, but average. Every now and then, I would gain a bit of confidence, only to be put back in my place.

In the fifth grade, Mrs. Wirtz saw something special in me. She convinced my parents to accelerate my mathematics. It lasted about two weeks. The whole fraction thing was really beyond mental comprehension. I remember my mother spending extra time with me at the kitchen table, trying her best to explain fractions. I got so frustrated and ended up in tears. I didn't understand it. My mom was kind and patient and said, "These are really complicated concepts. Fractions aren't for everyone. You'll learn it in time when you're ready, but you don't need to put this pressure on yourself. You're a very hard worker. You'll never be the smartest kid in school, but you'll be just fine."

Though I may not have been smart enough to figure fractions out, which precluded me from participating in more advanced academics, one area in which I always excelled was stubbornness. To this day, if I get something in my head, chances of me letting it go are slim to none. In the sixth grade, one of our assignments was to interview someone we admired. To get started, we brainstormed a list of people we admired. I still remember sitting in my classroom that day, staring at my blank piece of paper. All the other kids were vigorously writing down names. All I could think was, *How many people do they know?* Some kids had lists of three, some lists of 10 or more. And still, I just sat there, staring at my blank piece of paper. As Mrs. Clark made her way through the room, reviewing our sheets, I started to get nervous. She stopped at my desk and asked, "Why don't you have anything on your paper?"

"I really can't come up with anybody," I said.

"Well, what about your parents?"

I stared at her blankly. I liked my parents. I respected my parents. But the assignment was to come up with someone to interview whom you *admired*. Then I remembered my grandfather talking about his time working at the University of Iowa with Dr. James Van Allen.

Dr. Van Allen discovered the Van Allen radiation belts in space. I was fascinated by that. Here we are on Earth, and there are people out there, living in MY hometown, that MY grandparents know, who discovered something in space. Not only that, but the discovery was so profound they named these radiation belts (whatever they were) after him! Holy cow! There's somebody to look up to and admire. As Mrs. Clark walked away, I slowly wrote, "*Dr. James Van Allen*" at the top of my sheet.

At the end of the exercise, we took turns sharing with the class who we were going to interview. I remember one of the kids was going to interview a firefighter who was a neighbor of his. Another child planned to interview his mother, another her father, and another her uncle. All people close to them. I remember thinking, except for the fireman, those all sound boring. As my turn rolled around, I proudly declared, "I'm going to interview Dr. James Van Allen."

Aghast, Mrs. Clark responded, "Angie, Dr. Van Allen is a very busy and very important man. He doesn't have time for this interview exercise with a sixth-grader. You need to come up with somebody else."

I felt defeated. I went home in low spirits and told my parents what happened. "I guess I need to come up with somebody else."

Seeing the disappointment on my face, my mom said, "Or you could call Dr. Van Allen and ask him for an interview."

I just looked at her. "What do you mean?"

"Well, I'll bet his number is in the phone book. Look him up, pick up the phone, and call him. The worst he can say is no."

I thought, *Okay, I can do this. This seems reasonable. He does know my grandfather on my mother's side and my grandfather on my father's side, so it's not like I'm a complete stranger.* I went downstairs to the basement, where I could have some privacy. I picked up the phone and dialed the number, my heart beating in my chest. One ring. Two. And then a woman's voice on the other end of the line. "Hello?"

"May I please speak with Dr. Van Allen?"

"He's not home yet, but I can take a message and have him return your call. Who is calling?"

"My name is Angie Stochl," I replied. "I'm a sixth-grader at Robert Lucas Elementary, and we've been assigned a project to interview someone we admire. I'd very much like to interview Dr. Van Allen."

"Well, Angie," she said warmly, "I'll give him the message and have him return your call."

I was so nervous. I had butterflies in my stomach I'd never experienced before. Nervous anticipation flowed through me as minutes seemed to move in slow motion.

Later that evening, the phone rang. My mother answered and said, "It's for you." Wanting my privacy again, I rushed down the stairs to the basement and picked up the extension. "Hello?" I asked tentatively. A deep voice on the other end of the line replied, "Angie?"

"Yes, this is she."

"This is Dr. Van Allen, returning your call, and I would love to help you with your school project."

I was over the moon! I was so excited! Little did I realize I had closed my first big sale. I returned to school the next day and told Mrs. Clark, "Mrs. Clark! You're never going to believe it! I'm so excited! I called Dr. Van Allen last night, and he agreed to do my interview."

But instead of getting the congratulations I sought, I got a furious teacher. She was so upset. "Angie, I told you to come up with someone else and not waste his time."

I very meticulously prepared my interview questions. I researched everything I could about the radiation belts. On the day of the interview, my dad dropped me off at Van Allen Hall. Proudly, I went in myself and found his office on my own. I sat with Dr. Van Allen for about 45 minutes while I went through all of my questions. Wisely, my parents had suggested I take a tape recorder and record the interview to help me write my report (since I still didn't know how to take shorthand) and for posterity.

I wrote the report, submitted it, and when the grades came back, she gave me a B, supposedly for misspelling one science term three different times. I was crushed.

To this day, I still believe the grade was more about disobeying the rules and guidelines that had been established. I bucked the standardized expectation. But it didn't matter. I learned something far more valuable.

I learned that when you're on a bus you didn't choose, chances are there will be someone trying to keep you in a certain seat. When you take a risk and move to a new seat anyway, there is no telling who you might meet or what you might learn.

Even then, I didn't believe I was smart. That success—that win—came from being stubborn, hard-working, and willing to risk rejection to make the ask. As I moved into 7th and 8th grades, that flash of gumption disappeared, and I returned to my average self, making B's and an occasional A. All that changed in about 6 minutes after math class one day.

As the bell rang and our class began filing out, Mr. Brems asked me to stay back. He told me to take a seat and very casually said, "Angie, I want to ask you something. Why are you getting a 'B' in my class?"

I looked at him, unsure, and replied, "A 'B' is a good grade."

"A 'B' is a good grade. It's a good grade for an average student. Why are you getting a 'B' in my class?"

Indignant (and still stubborn), I retorted, "A 'B' is not an average grade. A 'C' is average, so a 'B' is above average."

"Okay, fine, you're right," he said, frustrated. "A 'B' is slightly above average. But you still haven't answered my question. Why are you getting a 'B'?"

"Because I'm a 'B' student."

"Who told you that?" He asked quickly.

"My parents did."

He looked at me, puzzled, and said, "Tell me more about that."

I went on to explain that my brother was the gifted one, not me. I was a hard worker but not overly gifted at anything, and that was fine. I would make average grades, go to an average school, get an average job, live in an average house, get married to an average guy, have an average family, and live an averagely happy life.

When I finished, he lowered his head for a moment, as if deep in thought. I sat quietly and waited. When he raised his eyes to mine, he very calmly said, "You're not average. You're an 'A' student performing at a 'B' level. Get out of my classroom."

I just sat there, stunned, and stared at him. Then I quietly got up and slowly walked out of his classroom, making my way to Social Studies in a daze. Was it true? Was I really an 'A' student? Did I have more in me than I thought I did?

Our formative years are spent on a school bus, and who we become is largely formed by those on the bus with us. This was the first time in my life that I had an identity crisis. I didn't know who I was. Was I a 'B' student? Was I an 'A' student? I realized I had been listening to what others told me about myself and letting their voices shape who I was. What did I actually know about myself? I showed up late to Social Studies and got detention for being late without a pass. But I didn't care.

Imagine my parents' confusion when I burst through the door that afternoon, excitedly screaming, "Mom! Dad! Guess what? I got detention. But it's okay because I think I may not be living up to my full potential, and I can really use the extra time to figure it out." Of course, they thought I had lost it. I'm 43, and I'm still relatively confident that my parents think I've completely lost it at least once a year as I break through barriers and embark on new endeavors.

This moment in my life was ultimately a defining, pivotal moment. I started doing things differently, thinking about myself and my abilities differently, and asking my other teachers, "Do you think it's possible that I could get an 'A' in your class? What would I need to do? What would that look like?" I started asking for help, and from that day forward, I never made another B again—at least not for trying.

Lesson two: When you don't have confidence in yourself, borrow someone else's confidence in you until you have your own. I didn't know what kind of student I was. I didn't know what was going to happen if I tried something new. I didn't know anything about who I was, and I certainly didn't have the belief in myself that I was an 'A' student. But I knew Mr. Brems believed I was an 'A' student. It wasn't a conscious decision to borrow his confidence until I developed my own. It was something I did unconsciously. What I didn't know is how many times in the years to come, I would unconsciously (then one day, consciously) borrow other people's belief in me until I believed in myself.

Sometimes, when you reach for the stars, you fall and land on a cloud; and a cloud is a pretty great place to be. When we think about our choice of travel, sometimes it's not our choice at all. We may be stuck on a bus, unsure of how we got there to begin with. However, there are always other passengers who can help you get the most out of the ride, help you determine the next stop you need to make, tell you when to pull the cord, and set you on a new course. You just need to have the courage to listen to them, borrow their confidence, and take the leap—even when the destination isn't clear.

Lessons Learned:

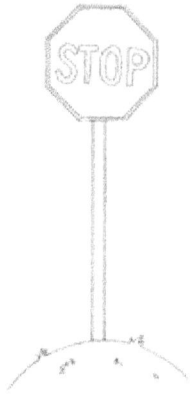

1. On any bus, there may be someone trying to keep you in a certain seat.

2. When you take a risk and move to a new seat anyway, there is no telling who you might meet or what you might learn.

3. When you don't have confidence in yourself, borrow someone else's confidence in you until you have your own.

CHAPTER THREE

This Is as Far as This Bus Goes

At some point in time, all buses have to return to the station. This pivotal moment forces you to choose which bus you will board next. When we think about our lives, the first major, pivotal choice in which most of us have a say is what we will do post high school graduation. Whether you are a first-generation college student completing your core courses at a community college, a legacy student heading to a 4-year university because it's a family tradition, or someone completing a vocational degree so you can begin earning a living wage to support your family, this is the first big decision most of us make.

The options available to us, however, have already been whittled down by determining factors like our grades, community involvement, access to funding, cultural/family support, and in my day, our ACT/SAT scores. While I had family support in pursuing higher education, my limiting factors were how I was going to pay for college and my ACT scores.

Most of my friends scored between 31 and 34 on the ACT the first time. I scored a 25. While I had gone nearly five years earning straight A's, I once again felt inferior. Stupid. Less than. I'd worked so hard between the 8th grade and my senior year to prove to myself that I was intelligent, capable, and academically competitive. I was a leader in the show choir, concert choir, madrigal choir, took dance classes, and taught dance to younger students. I played the piano proficiently, but somehow, I just could not score well on the ACT.

Having committed to Central College in Pella, Iowa, I needed a score of 27 to earn an academic scholarship. I didn't play any sports, wasn't involved in any clubs or volunteer activities, and had no idea how to research or apply for additional scholarship opportunities. If I could get that scholarship, my grandma (who had an 8th-grade education) would pay the difference. I studied in every spare moment I had. I have no idea how many practice tests I took. In the end, it took me four tries to make a 28. I was college-bound.

While I clearly was not the smartest or most talented of students, what I had going for me was that I was a hard worker who could focus on a single task for a prolonged period of time. My stubborn nature had evolved into a skill. Little did I know the hours of sitting at my piano, attempting to be the next virtuoso; the weekends and evenings I converted our game room into my own personal dance studio in the hopes of becoming the next Martha Graham; and the countless hours I poured over books into the wee hours of the night thinking maybe someday I would discover something cool in space like Dr. Van Allen would never bring me fame, fortune, or notoriety. I would never be an elite pianist, dancer, or scientist.

It turns out the elite skill I was developing was boredom. It wasn't piano, dance, or study that I was practicing all those years; I was practicing the art of sitting in boredom. As I reflect on it now, it is my comfortability in the boredom of repetition that has allowed me to succeed in nearly every endeavor of my professional career.

James Clear points out in his book *Atomic Habits* that, "Boredom is perhaps the greatest villain on the quest for self-improvement." When Mr. Clear realized his baseball career was over, he turned to a new activity: weightlifting.

He joined a weightlifting team, and one day an elite coach visited his gym. "What's the difference between the best athletes and everyone else?" He asked. "What do the really successful people do that most don't?" After listing the obvious attributes like "genetics, luck, and talent," the trainer responded, "At some point, it comes down to who can handle the boredom of training every day, doing the same lifts over and over and over."

This hit me like a ton of bricks. "That's me!" I shouted to absolutely no one in my bathroom one morning as I listened to *Atomic Habits* on the Audible app while getting ready for work. "I'm THE BEST at the boredom!"

When we reconcile ourselves to the fact that we may never be "the best," it becomes less about striving for the perfect outcome and more about striving for excellence in the process. It becomes about setting a goal, creating a plan, and executing the plan over and over and over until the desired outcome is reached.

Having made my first big life decision—which college to attend—it was time to make the next, even bigger decision. What should my major be? What do I want to be? I felt an enormous sense of pressure. Here I was, 18 years old, not exceptional at anything in particular, and yet it seemed my major would determine the rest of my life. Yikes.

From a family standpoint, I did not have a lot of guidance. My mom had worked for a loan and finance company for 20 years, and before that, she was a bank teller. My father worked in computer and software sales, where he sold computer and software systems to banks. Before that, he had been a loan officer at a bank and before that, a bank teller. My brother had been a bank teller. My grandfather had been a senior loan officer at a bank. As I looked around my universe of people I knew, my maternal grandmother worked at the same loan and finance company with my mother, and my grandfather owned and operated a junkyard. On my dad's side, my grandfather had passed, and my grandmother did not attend high school. There was not a plethora of diversity within the career sphere from which to draw when it came to my family.

Not only that, both of my parents had some college but hadn't graduated. My brother had gone to Texas A&M on a full-ride Air Force ROTC scholarship and had left after the first semester. I was the first person in my immediate family to be going to college, despite the fact that my maternal grandmother had earned her master's degree from the University of Iowa in 1952 and went on to become a teacher.

The only careers I knew anything about were banking, lending and finance, sales, and teaching. I desperately wanted advice from someone closer to and more familiar with the college experience than my parents, brother, or grandmother. So, I did what any normal, logical 18-year-old would do. I thought about the people I knew who had recently gone to college, graduated, and gotten what appeared to be successful jobs. One person, in particular, came to mind. His name was Greg, and he was friends with the son of some of my parent's friends. Never afraid of the phone, I called them and asked if I could have Greg's phone number. He had graduated from the University of Iowa, majored in business, and got a job at 3M in California.

I thought, *Well, this is obviously the right thing to do. I need to call Greg and ask him what I should major in so that I can get a good job and make a good living when I get out of college.* One night I was sitting at my desk in my room, staring at my piano phone. (You remember those, right? They were phones that looked like a grand piano, and each of the keys played a different note. I loved mine.) I picked up my sophisticated piano phone, called Greg, and said, "Greg, this is Angie Stochl. I'm going to college."

"Congratulations!" he declared.

"Thank you. But I don't know what to major in in college. That's the reason for my call."

There was a short pause on the other end of the line before he replied, "Well, let me ask you this: What are your favorite subjects in school?"

"Spanish, English, and public speaking."

"Well, there you go," he said definitively. "You double major in Spanish and Communication Studies."

I sat there for a minute and thought, *Oh my gosh, wouldn't that be so much fun? I could spend all day learning how to better communicate with people, learning how to speak in public and speak Spanish fluently.* I was picturing this wonderful college experience where I'm learning, growing, and blossoming, and then all of a sudden, my mind flashed to graduation, and my joy turned into panic. What kind of job does that lead to?

"Greg, what kind of job do you get with a double major in Spanish and Communication Studies?"

I will never forget his next words. "Angie, don't worry about it."

Laughing a bit, I said, "I can definitely do that, not worry about it. But you know my parents. You've met my parents. You know they're going to ask."

Very calmly and quietly, he said, "Here's the thing—major in something that you're passionate about. Others will see that passion in you, and the rest will work itself out."

It made so much sense to me. It was as though a light switched on in my mind. He's absolutely right. Why am I worried about what I'm going to do four years from now? All I need to do right now is go to college and be the best I can be at what I love. I thanked him for his time, hung up my piano phone, raced downstairs, and ran into the family room exclaiming, "Mom! Dad! I've got it! I know what I'm going to major in in college."

"What's that?" they asked.

"Spanish and Communication Studies."

They just stared at me. "What kind of job does somebody get with a degree in Spanish and Communication Studies?"

With supreme confidence I felt to the core of my being I said, "I don't know. But I'm going to be passionate about it. Others will see that passion in me, and the rest will work itself out."

Suffice it to say, my parents did not think this was quite the brilliant plan that I did, but I could not be deterred. As I reflected on the last 18 years, the times I dug my heels in—my interview with Dr. Van Allen, my determination to get straight A's, my stubbornness and commitment to scoring at least a 27 on the ACT—the reward had followed.

Lessons Learned:

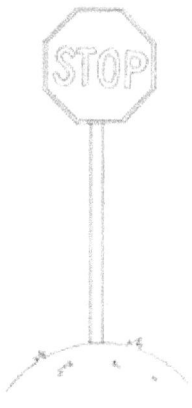

1. *Boredom is perhaps the greatest villain on the quest for self-improvement*

2. *When we reconcile ourselves to the fact that we may never be "the best," it becomes less about striving for the perfect outcome and more about striving for excellence in the process.*

3. *Be passionate about what you do. Others will see that passion in you and the rest will work itself out.*

CHAPTER FOUR

Chartering Your Own Bus

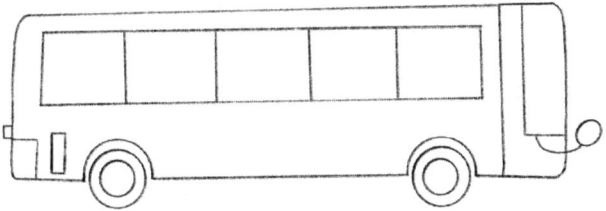

Most of my fellow graduates attended the University of Iowa or Iowa State University. Some went out of state, a few to smaller, in-state private colleges, like me. College felt like the first time I was breaking free, spreading my wings, and embracing who I was. It was a chance to start over socially and academically. I could be whoever I wanted to be, and this was my time to begin defining myself.

After my first meeting with my college advisor, I discovered that to make my academic plans work, which included spending a year abroad in Spain, immersed in the language, I was going to need to shift my abroad year up to sophomore year as opposed to junior year when most students study abroad. I also wanted a full year, not a semester. While nearly 30 percent of college students spend one term abroad, fewer than 8 percent of students commit to an entire year.

That went over like a lead balloon with my folks. But for the first time, there really wasn't much they could do about it. When the high school bus reached its final destination at the station, I chartered my college bus, and my parents were not on it. My tuition was covered, I had money in savings, and there was no stopping me.

I spent 1999-2000 in Granada, Spain, taking more dance classes than I did academic courses, thanks to my parents who helped me get the most out of my experience despite their earlier reluctance. It was the best year of my life. Like most kids who spend a year abroad, I returned home, changed. My worldview was so much bigger than it had been when I left, and I became obsessed with devouring information. As my junior year began, I took classes I needed to complete my requirements for my majors, but I needed more credits to earn my liberal arts degree. Rather than staying in my chosen fields of endeavor, I started taking classes that had nothing to do with my majors.

Then it happened. I picked up a political science class, mostly for fun, and while I know this is going to sound crazy, one day, I felt something click in my brain. Something shifted. I physically felt it. I looked up, pausing for a moment to see if anything hurt. Nothing did. I looked down at the text in front of me that, moments ago, seemed complicated. It didn't seem complicated anymore, and I thought, that's strange. I left poly sci, made my way to my next class, and the same thing happened.

I had always struggled with absorbing content (part of the reason I was so bad at standardized testing), but now when I looked at words on a page, it was as though my brain was processing them in a new, digestible way. All I can say about that moment is that it was the moment I learned how to learn. Having a college degree is great, but more importantly, is the ability to learn and process information. I recently read an article that said one of the determining factors of success is one's ability to process information quickly. That day, in the fall of 2000, something clicked in my brain, allowing me to learn and process information in a new way. Like any new skill, it takes time to develop, and over the course of the last 20+ years, I have become more and more proficient, giving me an edge.

Finishing out my junior year, I knew I was going to be competing against every other student graduating from college, and I needed to get a meaningful internship to distinguish myself. My work experience was relatively limited and did not demonstrate my competence in my areas of study.

I got my first job at age 13, teaching dance classes after school for my dance teacher. When I was 15, I went through the "Leaders in Training," or LIT, program at my church camp, Camp Wyoming. I loved LIT. I was a volunteer counselor for four weeks that summer - one week for church campers, one week for special needs camp (adults with intellectual and developmental disabilities), and two weeks for Tri-T camp.

Tri-T was a women's sorority that sent underprivileged, 10-year-old girls to camp for a week during the summer. I learned two very valuable lessons that summer that have never left me:

1. Every human with an intellectual or developmental disability—no matter how severe—has at least one gift or skill that far exceeds anything I will ever accomplish. It might be compassion, artistic skills, math, the ability to express unconditional love or tongue twisters, but I learned that special needs people are just like you and me, only with extremes. While I may have more balance in my abilities, I am not extremely gifted in any single ability.

2. You can change the course of someone's life through simple actions or words.

During one of my Tri-T weeks, there was a little girl named Monica in my cabin. It took six hours her first day of camp to get all the lice out of her hair and get her clean. She was a nightmare. That's the only way I could think to describe her. Difficult, negative, fought with the other girls, stole from them, mouthed back, you name it.

I did my best to be kind to her all week, but by the time Thursday rolled around, I could not wait for that week to be over.

I was walking up to the showers that morning with Monica and two other girls when one of the girls said, "I'm going to miss you, Miss Angela."

"I'm going to miss you, too," I replied.

"Whatever!" Monica said angrily. "You're only here because you're getting paid to be here."

I just laughed. "I'm not being paid! I'm a volunteer."

She stopped, dead in her tracks, and stared at me. "You mean you're here because you just want to spend time with us?"

"Yes," I said simply.

Tears filled her eyes. "No one has ever wanted to spend time with me before." Her towel and shower caddy fell to the ground as she lunged at me, wrapping her arms and tiny body around my waist in a big hug. I held her until she let go, then took her hand, picked up her things, and headed up to the showers. She did not leave my side and was the perfect camper from that moment on. My heart broke when she got on the bus to return home. I could not imagine what she must have been returning to.

After that, I was determined that I was going to go back to Camp Wyoming to be a full-time, paid camp counselor during the summers after my sophomore, junior, and senior years of high school. In the spring of my sophomore year, my parents asked, "What are you going to do this summer for work?"

I just looked at them like, Are you crazy? "I'm going to go to Camp Wyoming to be a camp counselor. That's why I spent last summer in LIT."

Definitively and united, my parents said, "There is no way you're going to Camp Wyoming to be a camp counselor."

"Why not?"

"You're 16 years old. You need to get a real job."

That's how I ended up a bank teller at First National Bank in downtown Iowa City, Iowa (because every single 16-year-old needs to be accountable for $26,000 in her drawer every day). I was a bank teller after my sophomore, junior, and senior years of high school, on Saturdays during the school year, and again during summers and holiday breaks for the first part of my college career.

As my college years were coming to a close, I did not think that "camp counselor for three weeks," "bank teller," and "dance instructor" supported my academic choices or demonstrated leadership in a way that would be compelling to a prospective employer. Hence, I was determined to secure an internship that could set me apart from the pack.

I needed to be able to position myself in new and different ways. My college had an internship program in Washington, D.C., which I thought would be unique. In speaking with some of the other students who had participated in the program, they didn't feel they were assigned much responsibility. I was looking for something with a high degree of responsibility that would enhance my resume.

During my junior year, I took a leadership course with the president of my college, Dr. David Roe, and I absolutely loved that class. At the end of the course, Dr. Roe wrote each of us a note on an index card. I have moved thirteen times since graduating from college, and I still have that notecard in my desk drawer to remind myself of what someone else saw in me.

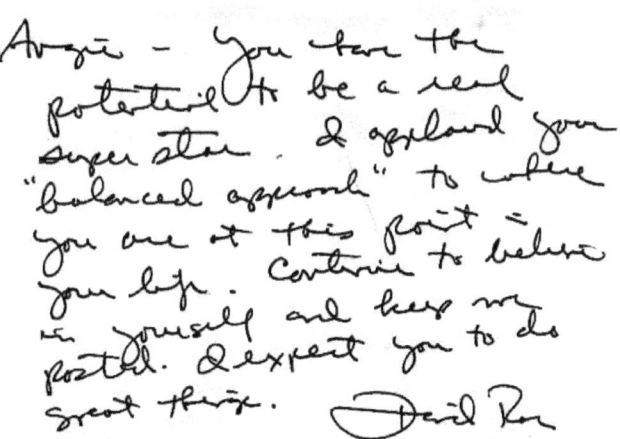

I went to Dr. Roe and said, "I'd very much like to do an internship in D.C. I know you're ex-military, I know you used to live in D.C., and I'm wondering if you know anyone who may be able to help me get an internship out there."

Respecting my boldness in asking for something I wanted and advocating for myself, he helped me get an internship at Cassidy & Associates in Washington. When I shared the news with my parents, I was met with a now familiar response of something to the effect of "Are you out of your mind?"

At this point, I had figured out that there wasn't much they could do to stop me. I went on Craigslist, found an apartment, and rented it. Knowing I would not be deterred, my mom said, "Okay, slow down. If you're determined to do this, I'm at least flying out there with you to make sure you're not renting from a psycho. I don't want you to end up dead."

That summer, I worked with one of the largest lobbying firms in the nation and learned so much about lawmaking, legislation, and impact. When the lobbyists at my firm learned I was from Iowa, "Oh thank God," were the first words out of their mouths. They were working with the Iowa Corn Growers Association and automatically assumed I was a farm kid with a depth of knowledge in ethanol. I am from Iowa City, Iowa, had not spent even one day of my life on a farm, and knew next to nothing about agriculture, let alone ethanol.

I did not have the courage to confess my ineptitude, however. The words, "Sounds like the perfect project for me!" came flooding out of my mouth before I could stop them. My next phone call was to my father, begging him to give me the phone numbers of some of our farming friends so that I could quickly get up to speed and not embarrass myself or my firm. It was truly a fascinating experience. I knew then that with the ability to learn, the humility to ask for help, and the bravery to advocate for myself, there was nothing I couldn't do.

Rolling into my senior year, I only needed 21 credits to graduate from college. I could graduate early and begin the independent life I had been striving for since I was in the eighth grade. I was so eager to be finished, but students were not permitted to take 21 hours without the President's approval. Once again, I found myself back in Dr. Roe's office, asking for an exception.

"I think you've sufficiently proven yourself in your time here," he said. "You're capable of taking one additional class."

I took 21 hours the fall semester of my senior year, packed up my room, and returned home in December. Once again, the bus pulled into the station—its final destination. That was as far as the college bus went, and it was time for me to embark on the next journey in life.

Lessons Learned:

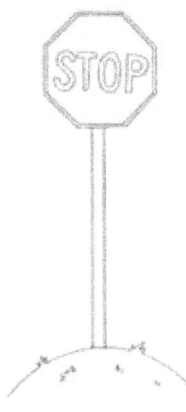

1. *Your ability to process information quickly is a major determining factor in your success.*

2. *You can change the course of someone's life through simple actions or words.*

3. *We all need to be reminded, from time to time, of what others see in us.*

CHAPTER FIVE

Let Me On!

As the college bus reached its final destination, it was time to select the next bus in my life journey. I knew additional higher education was not the right fit for me. I was eager to get into the workforce, start earning money, and begin my search for professional success (whatever that meant).

Principal Financial Group (now just Principal) was the largest employer in the state of Iowa in 2001. Because they are headquartered out of Des Moines, they actively recruited students from colleges all throughout Iowa.

My senior year, I was eligible for a preliminary interview with Principal. I had grown from the pimply faced, permed hair misfit of my youth into a confident young woman ready to shine. I had outstanding written and oral communication skills, and I was bilingual. I presented well and was confident. I thought for certain I would be a shoo-in for a job in marketing and communication. Many of my friends who graduated a year ahead of me had gone through this same interview process and secured jobs at Principal in marketing straight out of college. Not only that, my work study during my junior and senior years of college had been in the tutoring center. A few nights and weekend days a week, I would go to the tutoring center for open hours where other students could come in for help, specifically in English, Spanish, literature, writing, composition, communications, and some mathematics. I was more advanced than most of my peers and had a knack for explaining complex concepts in an easy-to-understand format. The same students I had tutored the last two years were the ones receiving job offers from Principal, so in my mind, my future with the firm was inevitable.

Imagine my dismay when I did not get a second interview. Instead, I received a rejection letter saying that I was not the right fit. All I could think was, *How is this possible? Everyone I've tutored for the last two years got a job there, but somehow, I'm not the right fit?* It made absolutely no sense.

Graduation came even though the job did not. I was so supremely confident that Principal would want me that I had not bothered to look for any other employment opportunities. And while I had absolutely no idea what I was going to do, one thing my parents made exceptionally clear was that I had a college degree; moving back home with them was not an option.

I look back on this moment in my life, and I see myself standing in the bus depot, my suitcase packed, looking at the big board of destinations. Step one: Pick a destination. The most logical location at that time was Des Moines, IA. Des Moines is the largest city in the state, and I reasoned, *It's not that far from home, the cost of living is reasonable (unlike Chicago), and surely there will be more opportunities there than anywhere else in Iowa.* And that was it. That was my entire decision-making process. Reluctantly, my parents helped me move to Des Moines. Because I was yet to be employed and had little credit, my parents had to co-sign a lease for me, but I was on my own. My rent and all expenses were my responsibility from that day forward.

Step two: find gainful employment (someone to let me on their bus). The world of employment had already shifted to online applications. I felt like I was standing in the bus terminal, looking at hundreds and hundreds of buses—all with open seats—knocking on doors and windows, hoping just one would open the door and at least allow me the opportunity to check out the accommodations.

I started applying for as many jobs as I could as I knew the money I had saved would not last long. Day after day I searched online for more opportunities. Every day my parents would call and ask, "Did you get a job yet?"

"No, but I applied for a few more online," I replied.

"You can't get a job online," they would retort. "You have to get out there and apply in person." This made no sense to me. I wanted to work for a professional company. It's not like they have signs hanging outside of office buildings saying, "Now Hiring."

"This is how you get jobs now, Mom and Dad. You apply online."

After about a month of grueling and tiresome conversations with my parents, I finally got a call from a small data processing company called "Premier Systems Incorporated," or PSI. They offered data processing services to credit unions. If you have ever seen the 1999 cult classic, "Office Space," it was basically just like that. I interviewed and was hired for a job as support staff for their sales team. Day one, I realized I had no idea what working in an office environment was like.

Growing up, the small company my mom worked for had two locations, neither of which consisted of more than three rooms and a storage closet. My mother's coworkers were her boss, Arnie, my grandmother, and Liz, a front desk worker. It was a tiny, casual, family-oriented environment. My dad was a traveling salesman. His car and our basement were his environments. Consequently, between my father and my mother, I had no idea what the unspoken rules of the workplace were.

I was fortunate to be befriended by a woman who was a little bit older than me on my first day at PSI. Her name was Melissa Rounds. She was kind, friendly, had a huge smile, and an infectious laugh. She is one of those people who makes you feel like you are the most interesting person she's ever met when you talk to her. Occasionally I would walk past Melissa's cubicle, and she would swing around in her chair and say cheerily, "Hey, how are you? How's your day?" or "How was your weekend?" It wasn't long before I looked forward to those conversations so much that I would intentionally stop by her cubicle daily.

At first, we chatted for one or two minutes. Then it was maybe five minutes. Then it got to the point where I was spending nearly 30 minutes a day talking to Melissa about things going on at work, in my personal life, and in her personal life. She was just always so kind and made me feel seen as I searched for my place and purpose within PSI.

One day, Melissa did something brave and exceptional. As I stopped by her cubicle, expecting a long chat to ensue like normal, she looked me straight in the eyes and said, "Angela, I really enjoy talking to you. I think you're a great person, but we can't talk for 30 minutes every day. It's disrespectful to our employer. We're getting paid to be here. And it's really disrespectful of my time because I have a lot of projects that I need to manage and get done, and I'm sure you do as well. It's not that I don't want to talk to you, but we need to be more respectful and do that over our lunch hour or before or after work to ensure we can both get our work done."

I was completely taken aback. I remember looking at her and saying, "Absolutely, I understand. Thank you." I felt embarrassed and like I had gotten in trouble. At 21 years of age in my first professional job out of college, I hadn't given much thought to what I was doing. I felt terrible, realizing that she was entirely right. I had wasted her time and company resources. I put my head down and started working harder than ever in an effort to make up for what I had abused. I also became more aware of my conversations and interactions with others, limiting them to appropriate standards.

To this day, I'm incredibly grateful to Melissa for giving me professional feedback. I didn't realize it at the time, but I look back on it now and realize the courage it took. I imagine her talking to her husband, Gregg, about her conflict the evening before over dinner, laying out a plan. Most people in her situation would have just started ignoring me simply to avoid conflict. Her willingness to have a difficult conversation changed my perspective and empowered me to give others critical, constructive feedback throughout their careers. One of my favorite expressions is, "If I knew better, I would do better." We don't always know better unless someone takes the time to teach us.

Working at PSI was a great experience, but my desire to work for Principal had not gone away. I still very much wanted to find employment with them. Much of that desire stemmed from the cultural values I was raised with. I was raised to believe that loyalty to an employer, above all else, gives you value and respect. A career with Principal would offer me benefits, growth opportunities, and the chance to work nearly my entire career with one employer.

Never deterred from a goal, I submitted a resume to Principal almost once a month for about a year. Finally, I received a call from a human resources professional saying, "We've received all of your email and resume submissions. We don't think you're qualified for any of the jobs you've applied for." My heart sank. Was this it? Would I never get on the Principal bus?

"However," the HR Representative went on, "there is one position for which we think you may be a match, but it's nothing you have applied for." My heart lifted ever so slightly and as she began describing the job, excitement began building inside me. It was right up my alley. People in this position traveled around the country, giving presentations on 401(k)s for Principal's largest clients. They needed presenters who could present in both Spanish and English. It was like manna from heaven! It was my opportunity to use my communication skills, my public speaking skills, and both languages to advance my career.

When I asked how much travel it was, they said 40 percent. At that particular point in my life, I was in a relationship, planning on getting married. Since my dad traveled so much when I was a kid, I really knew what 40 percent felt like, and I knew the toll it could take on a relationship. It is in my nature to place relationships ahead of any other personal or professional desire, and with great sadness and disappointment, I told the HR representative that because of the travel, I probably wasn't interested in the job. Later that day, when I shared what had happened with my boyfriend, he said, "What's the harm in interviewing?" I thought, *You know what? You're right*. There's never harm in interviewing. Maybe they won't even offer me the job, but it's a good experience. The next day I called back. "I know I said I wasn't interested because of the travel, but I changed my mind. Could I still have the opportunity to interview?"

> This is something I think people miss. Just because the door to the bus has closed does not mean it has left the station.

Just because you say "no" to something initially doesn't mean the opportunity has vanished. The door may be closed, but you always have the option of knocking. The worst outcome is they tell you no, and you're in the same position you were in before. The best outcome is they are still willing to give you another chance.

Thankfully, the Principal bus had not made its final boarding call, locked its door, or left the station, and I was permitted to interview for the job, though I was told it was rather unorthodox. The reason for the exception became clear in the interview.

Apparently, Principal had signed a large, new client to its retirement platform and was in desperate need of Benefit Service Representatives to onboard the client. There were several interviews, but the one that counted the most was the personal presentation.

Candidates were tasked with creating a PowerPoint presentation on our qualities and why we were the right person for the job. I am certain I still have that presentation on a floppy disk somewhere, but what I remember most is walking into the meeting room, six to eight people sitting at tables in a U-shaped configuration, and me, standing in the middle of the room, pitching myself. It was equal parts nerve-wracking and exhilarating!

Days later, when they called and offered me the job, I experienced my first professional adrenaline rush. It was the same feeling I had when Dr. Van Allen had agreed to my interview request. I was so proud. With determination and tenacity, I secured a job with the employer of my dreams and directly applied my degree to my future work. I had followed Greg's advice and belief in me and it had worked! I had been passionate. Others had seen that passion in me, and the rest was working itself out. I had done it!

The first call I made was to my parents to tell them the great news. With enthusiasm, I told them how I was going to be traveling around the country, doing exactly what I went to college for—public speaking and conducting meetings in Spanish and in English. When I finally came up for air, there was a long pause on the other end of the line. "We're so happy for you," they said. "But can we ask…what qualifies you to do this job?"

I felt like someone had burst my balloon. Feeling myself slowly coming down off my high, I responded, "I think the qualifications are that they need people who are good public speakers and bilingual."

"Yes, but you're only 23 years old. What do you know about investing and insurance?"

"Nothing," I responded. (Full disclosure: this seemed like a ridiculous question.) "I presume there's going to be formal training associated with this position to provide me with the knowledge and skills I need to fill the role. Regardless, they think I'm the right fit for the job. And if they believe it, I will prove them right."

Was getting a job different now than it had been when my parents had gotten jobs? Had they somehow already known how to perform all the tasks associated with their positions before they had even started? Their questions caused a bit of doubt to creep into my head, but once again, I would not be deterred.

I pulled the cord on the PSI bus, submitted my two weeks' notice, and made my first bus transfer. For me, this was not just a bus transfer; it was a bus upgrade. Going from this small data processing company in West Des Moines, Iowa, to working downtown on the Principal campus was a huge accomplishment for me. No one else in my family had ever worked for such a large or prestigious company. I felt like I had been called up to the big leagues. I felt like Tess in the movie, *Working Girl* (cue, "Let the River Run").

My first day of employment, I met the three other women who had been hired into the same role. Two of them were internal hires and already had their Series 6 license. The third was a returning employee, unlicensed, like me. I was the youngest of all four with the least amount of experience. We found out more about the new client that had just been signed to the Principal retirement platform and the need for us to get up to speed as quickly as possible to make the deadline for 401(k) enrollment, education, and understanding investing meetings.

I knew when I accepted the job that there would be licensing requirements, but I had no idea what that meant. I quickly came to understand it meant we had 60 days to earn our Life and Health insurance license, pass the Series 7 exam (also known as the General Securities Representative Exam: GSRE), memorize a 34-page script, and become comfortable delivering that script in front of a group of people.

If you fail the Life and Health exam, you only need to wait a week to retake it. However, if you fail the Series 7, you have to wait 30 days to test again. Because Principal really needed us up and running, we were told we had two chances only to pass the Series 7. If we failed on our first attempt, they would keep us on for another 30 days, but we had to pass the second time. If we didn't, our employment would be terminated.

Candidly, I had absolutely no idea what the Series 7 was and only a vague idea of what the Life and Health was. I was not, however, intimidated. I had learned how to learn in college and figured this would be no different. And let's be honest: if you have to learn something, what a great thing to learn. I was excited to become educated about how the stock market works. I wanted to know more about investing. I opened my first Roth IRA on my 18th birthday and wanted to be an educated investor. I remembered watching the ticker tape scroll endlessly on CNBC in my dad's home office, thinking how strange and nonsensical it all seemed. I was eager to crack that mysterious code and gain a skill that would benefit me my entire life.

Because this is a highly regulated industry, we were required to memorize the 34-page script word for word. Words matter in the world of investments and insurance because "and" versus "or" can make a huge difference in a potential lawsuit. We needed to be able to recite our lines effortlessly to keep from becoming flustered, present ourselves professionally, and to protect the firm.

During the workday, our supervisors coached us on memorizing the script and helped us with our presentation skills so that we could command the room. That meant our exam study time was at home, at night. We all decided to take the Life and Health exam first because it was supposedly easier. Wouldn't you know it, my three coworkers passed, and I failed. That put me one week behind in studying for the Series 7. After one additional week of studying for the Life and Health to ensure I would pass, I was left with one week of self-study for the Series 7 and a one-week class, paid for by Principal. I knew I needed to be scoring between 80 and 90 percent on practice tests in order to pass the actual exam. *I can do this*, I thought. I put my head down and spent as much time as I possibly could studying at night and on the three weekends I had to prepare. My test was scheduled for the Tuesday after I completed the class. I wanted to take it as soon as I could while everything I had jammed into my brain was fresh.

I had only taken two practice exams because the test takes 3+ hours to complete (you are allotted 3 hours and 45 minutes for the actual exam), and I had not scored higher than 65 percent on either of them. I was 100 percent certain that I was going to fail, and I was okay with that. I would have 30 more days to study and figure it out, and I knew that I could learn the material with the extra time.

On the day of my exam, it was absolutely gorgeous outside. I wore a black and white, velour tracksuit with a white tank top and tennis shoes. I was not the least bit nervous. Certain that failure was the only option, I was relaxed, comfortable, and in a good mood. *Treat this like a practice exam. Just do the best you can*, I told myself.

My exam started at 8:00 am. I finished the first half by 9:15, well ahead of my allotted time. Exam takers are given a break at the halfway point, and although it was too early for lunch, I thought, *Well, this is technically my lunch break.* I decided to treat myself to my favorite sandwich—the Herby Turkey from Bruegger's Bagels. With my belly full and taste buds happy, I returned for the second half of the test, still harboring no delusions of passing.

As I selected my answer to the very last question, my heart started to race. I hit submit, my heart now pounding, wondering, *What's going to happen? How bad did I do? 50 percent? 60 percent?* At least I would know which areas to focus on for the next test. It seemed to take an eternity for the score to be calculated, and then suddenly, there it was.

At that time, you needed a 70 percent to pass the Series 7. Right there on my screen, I stared blankly at the words: *Pass: 70 percent.* Surely there was some sort of mistake. There must have been a computer glitch. I got up from the computer and went back out into the testing center reception area. The lady at the front desk smiled brightly and said, "Congratulations, you passed!"

"Was it a mistake?" I asked.

Puzzled, she replied dryly, "No, you passed the test. You needed a 70 to pass, and that's what you got." I think she thought I was daft. She was probably wondering how I passed the test if I couldn't even read the score.

Stunned, I took the piece of paper she handed me and walked out into the bright sun in a daze. I picked up my phone and called my dad. "Dad, you're never going to believe this. I just passed my Series 7."

There was that long pause at the other end of the line again. Then my Dad asked, "You mean you're a licensed stockbroker?"

"No, I don't think so." *But the reality is that I was indeed a licensed stockbroker.* Sometimes not knowing what you're getting yourself into offers you the edge you need to succeed. Years later, I would hear countless stories from other brokers about their experiences in taking the Series 7. People told them how hard it was, how only 65 percent of people passed it on the first attempt. I also found out later that firms like Morgan Stanley and Merrill Lynch give their rookie brokers 90 days to study for the exam because it's so challenging. To me, it was just something I needed to complete in order to do the job for which I had been hired. Ignorance, certainty that I would not pass due to a lack of preparation, and the comfort of knowing I would be afforded 30 more days to study and retest helped me maintain a positive attitude and stay relaxed throughout the exam. And it paid off!

As our training progressed, I gained newfound confidence in myself and my ability to meet demands in a short period of time. Little did I know that the next passenger to get on my bus would give me the paving stones to begin building my road to success.

My parents were not entirely wrong when they asked me, "What qualifies you to do this job?" I was 23 years old and probably looked more like I was 18. My coworkers were all between 24 and 26 years old. This job required us to work with Principal's largest clients, their institutional clients. Institutional clients are classified as having $25 million or more in retirement plan assets. Because two of us were bilingual, the vast majority of clients that we went to see were manufacturing companies. As you can imagine, these are very, very valuable relationships for the firm. The concern was how young women would establish credibility and respect in front of 200 factory workers, many of whom are men, while giving presentations on enrolling and investing in their company's 401(k) plan. It was a valid concern. What did I know about saving and investing?

For years, Principal had contracted with Dr. Glenn Pfau to teach their employees professional image, communication, and public speaking skills. The training lasted for three days, and I tell you with all sincerity that having this opportunity early in my career accounts for somewhere between 50 and 75 percent of my professional success and much of my personal success. If I could give one piece of advice to anyone looking to advance their career—no matter how long they have been in the workforce—it would be to improve your image, communication, and presentation skills. Albert Mehrabian, a researcher of body language, first broke down the components of a face-to-face conversation. He found that communication is 55 percent nonverbal, 38 percent vocal, and only 7 percent words.

Dr. Pfau was probably in his 70s when I first went through his program. A retired Navy Seal, his methodology was to tear you down to build you back up. It wasn't just that he was teaching you how to command a room. He was teaching you how to *be a leader* from the moment that you walked in the door. He taught through principles.

At every seat, there was a white, blank notepad. The very first principle we learned was that leaders write in blue ink. Many people showed up with black pens. Others showed up with pink or green inked pens. He quickly put a stop to that. Leaders do not write in pink ink. Leaders write in blue ink.

His seminar was an attention-grabbing combination of observing him speak, writing down principles (which kept us active and engaged all day), watching video clips, and listening to passages from books that reinforced his message. Throughout the course of the three days, we got up in front of each other and gave several speeches. The first one we gave was short—less than one minute—about who we are, what our job is, where we come from, and one interesting thing about ourselves. Simple enough, right? He recorded us with a camcorder (for those of you born after 2006, camcorders preceded digital recording), making some brief, encouraging comments along the way. When we had all finished, feeling relieved it was over and fairly confident we had done well, he took the tape out of the camcorder and popped it into the VCR (which preceded DVD players and digital recordings) at the front of the room.

One by one, he began tearing us apart. It began with our clothing, our hair, our jewelry, and our shoes. Then he moved on to the way we talked, the tonality of our voice, our eye contact, and our fidgeting. He ripped into every single solitary part of us with no regard for feelings. He flat-out mocked us, made fun of us, and told us we were useless. Harsh? Yes. In fact, there was one woman in our group who actually left the room crying and nearly refused to come back.

By the time it was my turn to undergo his criticism, I had already learned that you can't take yourself too seriously. I thought I had been dressed sharply that day in a pair of camel colored, wool slacks from J. Crew that buttoned up the side, a black turtleneck sweater, and comfortable, practical leather shoes that velcroed, but were stylish (apparently, I actually thought the words "velcro" and "stylish" could be used in the same sentence when I was 23). He immediately pointed out that my pants were hanging off me, clearly too big. My shoes made me look like I had the feet of a duck, rather than those of a human, and why did I introduce myself by saying, "Hi, my name is Angela." Kindergartners say, "Hi, my name is." I was a grown adult. Did I not know who I was? Was I not proud of who I was? Leaders introduce themselves by saying, "Hi, I'm Angela," because being Angela means something. Angela has a brand, an identity. The verbal beating continued, and all I could do was laugh.

No matter how good we think we are, there's always room for improvement. There is always a way to get better. The best part about having room for improvement is that sometimes you can make huge strides with tiny choices, like your clothing selection or taking the time to polish your shoes.

Changing your wardrobe to be less distracting for your audience (solid colors, for example) presents you in a more professional manner, and it's not hard to do. How you speak—your pace, pitch, and power—how you enumerate on your fingers, how you make eye contact with your audience that is meaningful but not creepy, these are all skills he taught us. He mixed in his techniques with his set of principles. In the end, we had notepads filled with over 100 leadership and public speaking principles.

I had the opportunity to go through Dr. Pfau's training three times in my professional career. I have three notepads filled with leadership, speaking, and image principles that Dr. Pfau taught me. I have gone back to those notepads time and time again as I work to improve my leadership quality. I have added to the list and pared down some of the more technical speaking tips to create a list of about 55 key leadership and image principles that I strive to live by every day.

I've been told countless times that 55 principles are too many, and that I should just pick four or five. To that, I say, "You do you, and I'll do me!" I refer back to these principles at least once a month because of principle number five:

I CAN: <u>C</u>onstant <u>A</u>nd <u>N</u>everending <u>I</u>mprovement

No matter what bus you are on or which seat on the bus you are currently occupying, there is always room for self-improvement. The key is making the space and time in your life dedicated to improving. I was on the bus, in the right seat, packed, and ready to roll!

Lessons Learned:

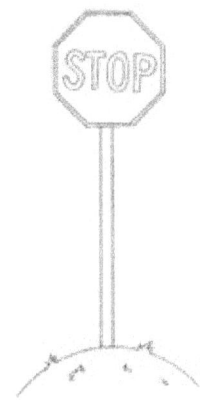

1. Having the courage to have an uncomfortable or critical conversation with someone can form the leader they become.

2. If I knew better, I would do better.

3. No matter how good we think we are, there's always room for improvement.

CHAPTER SIX

Traveling Alone

After Dr. Pfau's training, I felt well-prepared to embark on my journey. I had confidence in my presentation skills, my knowledge of 401(k) plans, and myself. However, I did not anticipate just how much I would learn about the world and its workings. Many of us are unsure of what we want to be when we grow up simply because we're unaware of what opportunities exist out there.

The world is incredibly vast. The most fascinating aspect of my job was discovering the intricacies of how things are manufactured and meeting the individuals responsible for creating them. Prior to this role, I hardly noticed the miles and miles of telephone cables connecting us across the United States, enabling communication. However, that changed when I visited Southwire Corporation in Heflin, Alabama, during my training trip. I never truly understood the process of jewelry-making until I conducted meetings for Sterling Jewelers in Akron, Ohio.

I was introduced to concepts such as stamping factories, clean workspaces for digital car components, and foundries. The highlight of my job became touring facilities, interacting with workers, and learning about the production of everyday products and services. My worldview expanded beyond what I had ever imagined.

This job also taught me a lot about social status. The role was challenging in that, to serve your clients effectively, you needed to provide the same level of education and enrollment opportunities to every employee, from the immigrant woman on the night shift to the dad working the second shift, all the way up to the executives. This also involved understanding the intricacies of various retirement plans, from union to non-union to executive plans.

In a typical week, I would leave Des Moines on a Sunday, usually taking a 4:00 pm flight. In 2003, our briefcase served as our overhead carry-on, while our projector became our under-the-seat carry-on. We all traveled in suits and heels, as we had to check our bags. This ensured that, in case our luggage didn't arrive, we would still be dressed professionally upon arrival. I vividly remember dashing through O'Hare, sprinting as fast as my 23-year-old legs could carry me in heels, clutching a briefcase filled with folders and lugging a projector the size of today's printers in a wheeled bag behind me to make most of my connections.

It likely won't come as a surprise to learn that there were few direct flights from Des Moines, IA, in 2003 and my route always included layover in Chicago. Once my final air destination was reached, I'd rent a car and drive an hour or two to the town in which the factory I was visiting was located. This was before GPS, so if you didn't remember to print MapQuest directions before leaving the office on Friday, you were at the mercy of incomplete car rental maps to guide you.

I'll admit that planning has never been my strong suit. I'm a dreamer, a visionary, a salesperson. My idea of "planning" a vacation is booking a flight and hotel. As a result, by the end of my time in this role, I had collected maps of 26 of the 50 states purchased at gas stations along the way. The upside to this is that, in an era where many people blindly follow Waze and Google Maps, I'm grateful I was forced to develop a sense of direction and the ability to read a map.

Upon arriving in the small factory towns I visited each week (or during the first part of the week, as it wasn't uncommon to start in Michigan, fly to Colorado or California, then return to Michigan before heading home on Thursday), it was typically around 8:00 pm. Despite not being much of a planner, I despise being late. Dr. Pfau taught us that being "on time" meant anywhere from 7 minutes prior to your appointment to 2 minutes after. Therefore, my first task was always to locate the factory where I would soon be conducting meetings. After finding the factory, I'd check into my hotel (or motel, in most cases) and sleep for as long as possible before the day's demands began, typically around 1:00 a.m.

The manufacturing client I worked with typically operated on three shifts: 7-3, 3-11, and 11-7. They also had Spanish-speaking only employees and English-speaking only employees. Meetings were scheduled at the end of shifts, during lunch breaks, or within the regular workday, depending on an employee's position within the social and socioeconomic hierarchy.

I would wake up around midnight to shower because, after a day of travel and a sprint through O'Hare, it always refreshed me. I arrived at all my meetings 30 minutes early, allowing me time to set up my projector and get oriented. For instance, I might set up a 2:00 am meeting at a lumber factory on the factory floor, projecting my screen onto a wall while workers sat on freshly cut lumber beams. At an automotive plant, I often found myself in the lunchroom at 3:00 am during workers' lunch breaks or shift changes, my projector perched on a trash can as employees sat at lunch tables. Once, during a visit to a turkey packing plant, I couldn't use the projector for the Spanish-speaking employees. Instead, I donned a long white coat over my suit, tucked my hair beneath a hairnet, inserted earplugs, donned plastic glasses, and covered my heels with booties to present to these employees on the kill floor, with turkey carcasses passing by on a conveyor belt throughout the presentation. Immediately after that meeting, I shed my turkey attire and headed up to the boardroom, where I quietly waited for two and a half hours for the executives to arrive, so I could conduct their meeting in the comfort of plush leather chairs and a long mahogany table.

My days had many extended breaks with no access to the Internet or cell phones that did anything beyond making calls. This afforded me plenty of time to read, which became one of my favorite pastimes. I distinctly recall reading *The Da Vinci Code* from start to finish in one night when I had meetings scheduled every two hours at an automobile factory somewhere in a flyover state. There wasn't enough time to return to the hotel and sleep, so staying at the factory and immersing myself in a captivating book (thank you, Dan Brown) seemed like the most logical choice.

The challenge, as you might expect, was getting enough sleep. I seldom managed a consistent seven or eight hours of sleep. Getting three hours of rest, followed by a shower, and then maybe six or seven hours of meetings before hopping back in the car for a 3 to 5-hour drive to the next location was the norm.

One trip remains etched in my memory. I had flown to Mobile, Alabama, conducted meetings in and around Daphne, had dinner, caught a few hours of sleep, then woke up at 11:00 p.m. to shower before hitting the road by midnight. I drove 4.5 hours up to some small town in central Alabama to set up at 4:30 for a meeting at 5:00 a.m. My mom was incredibly concerned about me driving through Alabama in the middle of the night, so she stayed up and talked to me on the phone for practically the entire drive.

Around 7:00 a.m., the woman in charge of human resources, who was the main contact for this client, entered the room, took one look at me, and said, "Honey, have you eaten?"

Her thick Southern accent was foreign to me. She sounded like a character straight out of a movie. "No," I replied.

"Well, come on!" she said, gesturing for me to follow her. "Imna [I'm going to] take you up to the country club. We got a real nice black lady up there and she gonna fix you up some grits."

I had no idea what grits were (we eat potatoes in Iowa) and I was pretty sure you weren't supposed to mention the race of the person making you breakfast (or anyone, for that matter). It was at this moment that I realized I was in the *South*.

As we drove through town, the woman pointed out various buildings, stores, and hunting areas she frequented. She was so kind, and I thought to myself, *This is what they mean by southern hospitality*. She introduced me to everyone at the country club. People were genuinely interested in meeting someone new—and from the North, no less. I was assured that no one would hold my northern roots against me.

After breakfast, we returned to the factory, where I conducted executive meetings, packed up my belongings, and began the 4.5-hour drive back to Mobile. I was staying one more night, would have a few more meetings the next morning, and then head back to Des Moines.

My meetings ran late, and I was racing against the clock to refuel the rental car, return it, and catch my flight on time. As I hurried through the airport, I heard them calling my flight. I made it just as the last passengers were boarding, stowed my briefcase in the overhead bin, slid my projector under the seat in front of me, and collapsed, exhausted, into my seat. I closed my eyes and drifted off to sleep in a matter of seconds.

The next thing I knew, someone was shaking me awake. It was a small regional jet, with two seats on either side of the plane and no first-class cabin.

"Excuse me, you're in my seat," a man in a dark suit with an equally dark expression snapped at me.

"What?" I looked at him, bewildered. Had the plane already taken off?

"You're in my seat. I'm in 3B."

"Oh," I muttered, pulling out my boarding pass. We were still at the gate. "My mistake. I'm in 3C, just on the other side of the aisle. Would you mind switching seats?" My assigned seat was immediately to my left.

"Yes, I would mind. You're in my seat."

"Okay..." I replied a touch sarcastically. I stood up, retrieved the projector from under the seat in front of me, took one step to the adjacent seat, placed the projector under 2C, and apologized to the man to my left.

"I'm sorry," I said.

"No problem," he responded. "I'm in the correct seat."

I offered a weary smile and closed my eyes. I was asleep again before the plane took off. Some time later, I woke up as the flight attendant came around with beverages. "I'll have a vodka martini," the man next to me declared. "And she'll have one too. I think she needs it."

His name was Dan Jensen, and he was fantastic. He lived in Kansas City but hailed from Des Moines, and he was traveling home to visit family. He had also been on business in Mobile. We conversed for the remainder of the flight, passed the layover in Memphis with more martinis, and vowed to stay in touch. Years later, I would relocate to Kansas City, and it was wonderful to already have a friend there. Dan was a tremendous help to me personally and professionally; he was always there to lend an ear, offer advice, and introduce me to important connections. What's more, Dan was an incredible cook. I never turned down an invitation to a party, dinner, or cocktail hour at Dan and Rick's home. You just knew it was going to be a fantastic time.

Dan was my first "airplane friend." It has been 20 years, and I still consider him a friend. Although our paths have diverged, I can't recall a day when we didn't have at least one game of Words with Friends going.

I enjoyed my role as a Benefits Service Representative. I relished learning new things and meeting remarkable people, but it was undeniably exhausting.

I had been crisscrossing the United States for about a year, wondering how much longer I could keep up the pace, when an incident in Cleveland made me question my personal safety on the job. I was scheduled to conduct a series of meetings in an industrial park that began at 2:15 a.m. Until that point, there had always been someone from Human Resources or an administrative department at the factory to meet me, regardless of the hour.

However, I had not succeeded in reaching the employer contact prior to my arrival in Cleveland.

After checking into the hotel, I tried calling the employer again, but no one answered. I phoned my boss and said, "Listen, I'm supposed to be at these meetings in about six hours, but nobody is answering the phone, and I don't know who's going to meet me there." My supervisor made a call and finally got through to someone. She called me back and said, "She's expecting your call."

I'll never forget the woman's response when I asked if she would be there to meet me at 1:45 a.m. "I'll be damned if I'm getting out of bed to meet you there at one in the morning. Just go around the back of the factory and see if you can find a trucker smoking a cigarette to let you in." I was 24 years old, 5 ft. 3 in. tall and weighed 110 pounds.

As I pulled into the dimly lit industrial park in the dead of night, I questioned the wisdom of my decision. Was this really the safest choice? I began to doubt the overall safety of the path I was on. If you were choosing between buses to travel across the country, would you opt for an old school bus lacking air conditioning, heat, and seat belts, driven by someone with questionable eyesight? Is that truly the wisest and healthiest choice you could make?

Reluctantly, I circled around to the back of the factory. Thankfully, there was a trucker outside smoking a cigarette, and he kindly let me in without incident. There are many good people in the world.

Every now and then, it's wise to consider the risks we're taking in pursuit of career advancement or goals, in general. Is it worth it? For me, it wasn't. I was exhausted, and even though nothing happened, driving alone to a remote industrial park in Cleveland in the middle of the night, with only the faint hope of encountering someone smoking a cigarette who could grant me entry to do my job, didn't rank high on my list of "wise decisions." That was the turning point.

Upon returning to Des Moines, I sat down with my boss and confessed, "Listen, I love this company. I appreciate the opportunity. But I'm tired. I don't know how much longer I can keep this up."

The average burnout period in my role was 18 months. I had made it to twelve months, and as I voiced my concerns about personal safety, she responded, "I understand. One of the remarkable things about you is your ability to achieve high enrollment rates and increase 401(k) plan contributions. I believe you would excel in a sales role." In essence, the job I had been performing was all about selling people on enrolling in their 401(k) plans and gradually boosting their contributions over time. I was flattered and taken aback by the fact that she thought highly enough of me to refer me to a sales department within our company called Principal Connection.

I was convinced that when I told her I was burnt out, my tenure at Principal would come to an end. What I didn't fully grasp at the time was that I was just a passenger on the Principal bus. I was living out what Jim Collins discussed in *Good to Great* as an employee. Right employee, wrong seat. I was a dependable, intelligent, dedicated worker. The company had invested considerably in my first year. It made more sense, both logistically and financially, to reposition me within a new department rather than let me go and start the process anew by recruiting and training someone else.

Over the past decade, I've witnessed employees leaving their jobs without even attempting to address their concerns with their employers. While not every workplace issue can be resolved, one lesson I learned from my experience at Principal is that it's not always necessary to pull the cord and switch buses. Open, honest, and respectful communication can go a long way and result in a simple change of seats on the bus—an opportunity to leverage your experience, and connect with other passengers.

Lessons Learned:

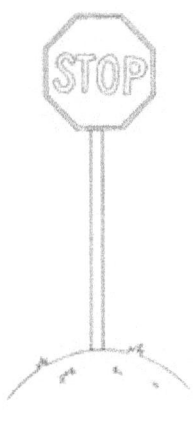

1. The world is a vast place full of jobs and opportunities you likely do know exist. Never turn down an opportunity to learn about something previously unknown to you.

2. Listen to your gut. There is no need to put yourself at risk–perceived or real–to advance professionally.

3. Reliable, hard workers are employees employers want to retain. Have the courage to have a conversation about your threads of discontent with a good employer before pulling the cord on the bus altogether.

CHAPTER SEVEN

The Rowdy Bus

Principal Connection worked with retirement plan participants when they separated from their employment. "Separation" meant they took a job elsewhere, retired, or were laid off, downsized, or let go. When an individual left their company and had more than $5,000 saved in their 401(k) plan with Principal, they received instructions to contact Principal Connection for help with what to do with the money they had accumulated in their plan. Our goal was to retain their assets at the firm by helping them roll over their 401(k) into an IRA, as well as to discover if they had other assets held outside Principal we could potentially consolidate at the firm.

Fun fact #1: Most people believe IRA stands for "Individual Retirement Account." In fact, it stands for "Individual Retirement Arrangement." Fun fact #2: The money you save in your employer-sponsored 401(k) plan isn't *technically* yours. Your employer holds the money in the plan, which means that if your employer faces financial challenges like bankruptcy or lawsuits, the plan assets (your money) could be frozen. This restriction prevents you from adjusting your investment mix, rolling over funds, or making withdrawals, regardless of market conditions.

Now, don't get me wrong—I'm a huge advocate of employer-sponsored retirement plans. However, once you're no longer with your employer, the smart move for most people is to transfer that money from your employer plan to your personal IRA as soon as possible! Since most individuals won't stay with one job their entire life, having a single account to consolidate funds from various employer-sponsored 401(k) plans just makes sense.

I was thrilled when Principal Connection offered me the job. It was an opportunity to learn more about investments and retirement planning while remaining with the company I had worked so hard to join. When I shared the good news with my parents, their first question was, predictably, "What qualifies you for this role?" A pattern was starting to emerge.

"I have absolutely no idea, but they clearly think I can do it."

Their question did not fill me with as much doubt this time as it had the last. I had learned Principal did, indeed, have great training. I had become proficient in my last role and anticipated success in this role. Walking into my new sales position, I felt confident. My former boss believed in me, the hiring managers believed in me, and despite my parents' concern, I believed in myself.

Belief in your abilities, it turns out, was not enough. During the first several months, I consistently ranked among the bottom five performers in my department. There were approximately 60 people in Connection at the time, and we received daily reports highlighting how much money each of us converted from 401(k)s to IRAs and how much money we consolidated from external firms. At the end of each month, the final ranking report came out. You always had an idea of where you stood based on the daily reports, but there were always a few surprises at month-end.

Every single day and month, I found myself among the bottom five producers. I struggled to convince people to roll over their money. They often cashed out, transferred funds to other firms, or left the funds in their former employer's 401(k) plan, even if they no longer worked there (which, as previously established, was generally a poor choice). Each month, I underwent "Call Performance Reviews" (CPRs) with my supervisor. Since our calls were recorded, she spent an hour reviewing calls and offering feedback. Every month, she highlighted my mistakes. Eventually, I began to believe my parents were right—I was unqualified for the job, unable to perform, and a failure. These doubts consumed me, and the nights before my CPR, I struggled to sleep. I cried before I went to work and as soon as my CPRs were over, I retreated to the bathroom where I cried even more.

It was an agonizing experience, and I grew increasingly unhappy. I tried giving myself pep talks, but every time I managed to get my adrenaline going I would make some stupid mistake. I remember one morning in particular, telling myself, *You can do this. You got this!* I arrived at work at 7:50 am, logged in promptly at 8:00 am (when calling and receiving calls was allowed), and reviewed my lead list—a roster of individuals who had left their jobs but hadn't yet contacted us about their account. *Today's the day,* I thought. With utmost confidence, I dialed the first number on my list, eager to impress.

"Hello?" a groggy voice answered on the other end.

"Mr. X?"

"Yes?"

"This is Angela Stochl calling from Principal Financial Group about your 401(k) plan."

"Do you know what time it is?" he asked.

"Yes, sir, it's 8:02 a.m."

"Maybe where you are. I'm in Hawaii. It's the middle of the night. Don't call me again."

Click.

What a rookie mistake! I hadn't even considered the time zone. I couldn't do anything right. Worst of all, this wouldn't reflect well in my next CPR. My self-doubt—that voice in my head telling me I was no good, that I did not belong here, that I was an imposter—got louder and louder. I was certain I would soon be unemployed, penniless, and homeless.

On the day of my scheduled CPR, something unexpected happened. My boss was absent and Jon Goergen, another supervisor, filled in for her on my CPR. I barely knew Jon beyond exchanging pleasantries. He was soft-spoken, kind, and attentive. Before we began, I said, "There's something you should know."

"What's that?" he asked, genuine concern on his face. His interest caught me off guard. I proceeded to recount my outbound call blunder. He looked at me for a moment, his face unreadable.

"Will you make that mistake again?"

"Absolutely NOT!" I declared emphatically.

"Well, then I think that was a valuable lesson learned."

With that, we moved forward. As we listened to calls together, rather than telling me everything I did wrong, he pointed out all the things I was doing right. It turned out that there were several things at which I was excelling. Occasionally, he'd pause a call and inquire, "Why didn't you say [this] here? Why didn't you say [that] there?"

"I wasn't entirely sure," I admitted.

"You know, I've been observing you since you joined us," he said. "People frequently approach you with questions about our products and investments."

"Yes," I acknowledged nonchalantly. "I prioritize product knowledge; it's important to me."

"So, why are you hesitant to share that knowledge with the people on the other end of the line?"

"I'm only 24 years old. They have more life experience and have been investing in these plans for a long time. I worry that maybe I shouldn't be the one giving them advice."

He pondered for a moment. "Let me ask you something. Who in this department cares more about people than you do?"

What an awkward question! If I said no one, would I sound conceited? "I don't think there are many who care about people more than I do, in general."

"That's what I think, too," he agreed. "Now, let me ask you this. You hold Series 7, Series 63, Series 65, and Life and Health licenses. You're a knowledge sponge. You're more well-versed in our products and services than 90 percent of the people here. When you're speaking to these individuals on the phone, who do you think understands investing and investments better? You? Or the guy who's been working in a stamping factory for 50 years?"

A light bulb switched on in my mind. "I do."

"Exactly!" he affirmed. "And because you care deeply about people, you'll never do anything to harm them. Right?"

"I certainly hope not!"

"You won't. You're meticulous about research, and you take time to really get to know people and understand their goals, risk tolerance, and objectives by asking insightful questions. Your only aim is to assist them."

"That's true," I acknowledged, my spirits lifting.

"So. Who can better guide them—you or someone else?"

"They're in better hands with me," I asserted, wholeheartedly believing it.

"All right, then. Let's go with that."

That was the end of my CPR that day. My entire perspective shifted in a matter of about 15 minutes, yet again broadening my horizons. He had given me a new script about myself and in doing so, gave me the mental freedom to focus on what the caller was saying rather than focusing on my own insecurities or fear of failure. He taught me that if I listened carefully to what the caller needed and wanted to accomplish, I could respond in an engaging, thoughtful, and compassionate way and success would naturally follow.

It was as if I had moved from one side of the bus to the other. Instead of staring mindlessly at nothing but gray rock, as if my window faced the side of a mountain, a beautiful landscape of lush, green trees and blooming flowers in every color of the rainbow spanned before me. My rise in the department's rankings began that very day. I understood that to realize my full potential, I needed to remain on this side of the bus where the horizon stretched ahead. Looking back, I recognize that my lack of confidence had been inflamed by repeatedly being told what I was doing wrong. While I believe my manager had the best intentions, employees are like children. No two are the same and they all respond to coaching differently. Leaders must learn which communication style resonates best with each individual employee, what will motivate them to reach beyond what they have already accomplished, and most importantly, what will empower them to take ownership over their own growth.

I approached our department head and requested a transfer to Jon's team. The process was simpler than anticipated. Despite preparing a lengthy explanation, I only needed to state that Jon's coaching style aligned with my learning preferences, and I believed I would excel under his guidance. In retrospect, Dean likely found the decision easy. After all, I couldn't perform any worse. There was no harm in changing my seat on the bus to assess if I still held value.

Within a month, I had climbed to the top half of the department, and within three months, I ranked among the top 10. Jon's coaching style proved effective for me. Soon after, Jon relocated my desk closer to his cubicle, and I joined an exceptional group of individuals in a new bullpen. I had a fresh set of fellow passengers—the rowdy passengers! Kyle, Nick, Jeff, and I had a blast every day. We worked hard, we held each other accountable, and we learned from one another. Most importantly, we laughed. A lot! We found ways to have fun in the monotony of phone call after phone call. The learning curve became less steep because I listened to what they said to clients, how they explained products and concepts, and how they positioned our firm.

My performance continued to improve, and I genuinely loved my job. There's something incredibly gratifying about being part of a team that consistently uplifts you, stands by you when deals fall through, and helps you identify where you went wrong so you don't repeat the mistake. It was an amazing experience; one for which I remain deeply grateful. Looking back, I still consider it the most enjoyable role I've ever held.

Lessons Learned:

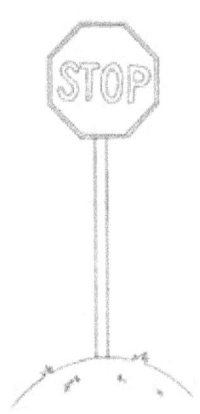

1. *Leadership consists of thousands of little things that make a big difference.*

2. *No one cares how much you know until they know how much you care.*

3. *Smile, chuckle, laugh, and joke.*

CHAPTER EIGHT

New Passengers

Traveling by bus, unlike by air, involves frequent stops—people get off, and new passengers get on. At this stage of my journey, a passenger boarded who would gradually and systematically take over the bus. For simplicity, let's call him "the sinister passenger." He would dictate my seat, the bus's destination, and all the passengers on board. However, this book is neither a confessional nor a tell-all. What I have to say about the subsequent buses I attempted to board, and ultimately boarded, is this: Be cautious about who's steering the bus, its trajectory, and their motivations for having *you* on board.

After approximately a year in my Principal Connection role, the firm introduced a pilot program, extending Principal Connection into the field. Face-to-face meetings with plan participants would be offered, rather than a phone-only option through our call center. The inaugural site for this pilot was New York City.

The sinister passenger and a few individuals at Principal believed I might be an ideal candidate for the role. I interviewed and was selected as one of the very first employees to pilot this program. This opportunity seemed enormous and had the potential to propel me into a senior leadership position one day. It was a bus I was equal parts nervous and honored to board.

Unfortunately, sharing the news with my parents about relocating from Des Moines to New York City did not go smoothly. This time, it wasn't solely about my qualifications for the job. Sometimes personal relationships clash with professional advancement.

The sinister passenger was pushing hard for me to accept this pilot role and I faced one of the toughest decisions of my life. I realized I couldn't sacrifice my relationship with my parents for professional gain. This decision not only caused a significant conflict with the sinister passenger but also led to a less-than-favorable response from the hiring manager when I contacted him to explain my withdrawal from the position due to personal reasons.

"I will ensure that you never receive another promotion at this firm ever again." There are consequences to pulling the cord on the bus too soon. I had eagerly accepted the job without fully considering the potential personal fallout. Presented with a choice between a risky professional move and preserving a meaningful relationship, I opted for the latter.

I began to recognize that everyone in my life had expectations of me—my parents, the sinister passenger, the firm. By nature, I am a people pleaser, even more so at that time than today. Given the chance, I would prioritize others' needs and desires over my own 99.9 times out of 100. In this scenario, there was no way to satisfy everyone, and unfortunately, I ended up being the biggest loser.

My home life became challenging, my parents were hurt, I missed out on a significant job opportunity, and I wasn't sure if another chance would come my way. I rededicated myself to my work in Principal Connection, focusing on enjoying my colleagues and striving to excel in my current role.

In December 2022, I had the privilege of meeting Jack (Jackie) Burke, a World Golf Hall of Fame Member and 1956 Master's Champion, just before his 100th birthday. When he inquired about my golf game, I replied, "It could use some improvement." He reflected for a moment and then offered, "The trick is to focus on what you are doing, not on what you're not doing. If you're putting and you're thinking, 'If I make this putt, I win the championship,' then you've already lost. You're not winning the championship! You're putting!"

As I reflect on it now, I focused on what I was doing: helping people take charge of their retirement assets and create plans to achieve their desired retirements. I didn't dwell on what I wasn't doing: earning a promotion.

Fortunately, that hiring manager must have lost his resolve. I was presented with another opportunity later in 2005 and transferred to the Kansas City field office as an Assistant Producer Development Coordinator.

The title was lengthy, but it essentially meant I worked with the Branch Manager to facilitate growth in that office's production (revenue).

One of the initial tasks assigned to me was networking and recruitment. At twenty-five years old, I was petrified at the idea of networking. First, I had no idea what it was. Second, my age played a major role in my apprehension to begin "schmoozing" with what I considered to be older, more seasoned professionals. As a young woman in the insurance industry, I was a minority. It's one thing to be a voice on the other end of the line; it's quite another to represent a prominent, professional firm in the community while attempting to recruit insurance agents, many of whom were men in their 40s and 50s, to join our team. I was deeply concerned about not being taken seriously and felt ill-equipped to be an effective networker.

Thankfully, much of my demeanor was shaped by the training opportunity I had with Dr. Pfau. Even though I lacked internal confidence, I projected an air of self-assuredness and intelligence externally. To this day, when I envision myself from within, I still see the skinny fifth-grader with a perm, acne, and braces. I endured my share of teasing. It hurt. I'd return home from school in tears over cruel remarks from classmates, and I recall my mom consoling me on the steps. "I have some bad news," she'd say. "Things don't necessarily improve. Many people never outgrow high school."

Was it comforting at the time? Not particularly. Yet, looking back, it's part of what fueled my determination to be knowledgeable. It didn't matter if I was attractive or wore designer clothes; my expertise and capability were valuable. I was a bit of a late bloomer and, to this day, I sometimes catch a glimpse of myself in the mirror and momentarily wonder who's in the bathroom with me. It's especially startling when I'm home alone! Internally, I'll forever be that awkward, unpopular fifth-grader. She fuels my ambition.

One day at an Overland Park Chamber of Commerce meeting, I met a woman named Breandan Filbert (we're still Facebook friends). She was the most outgoing person I had ever met in my whole life. She had a gregarious and infectious personality and was willing to help anyone. At that time, she offered a networking course that I decided to enroll in. If memory serves me right, the course cost $950, which was a substantial amount for me at twenty-five. However, I recognized that to add value to my boss, and learn effective recruiting and networking skills, I needed to step out of my comfort zone. It marked my first investment in myself. Through this experience, I discovered that networking was essentially an extension of what I had been doing all along.

To many people, "networking" is almost a dirty word. It conjures up the idea of using people to get something self-serving. I felt the same way before Breandan's course. I won't profess to remember everything I learned, but there was one tactic she taught that I have carried with me every day of my life since then. When meeting someone new, there are only 3 questions I need to ask:

1. What is your name?
2. What is something you are working on?
3. How can I help?

These three questions accomplish more than we have time for in this book, but in essence, they allow you to quickly learn who you are talking to (their name), what is important to them (do they share something they are working on in their personal or professional life?) and if what you have to offer (your knowledge, skills, connections, etc.) aligns with what they are seeking (can you actually help?). From there, you can make an informed decision about whether the conversation and relationship is worth pursuing. This made networking seem less seedy and much more interesting. It was empowering.

Asking questions and actively listening, rather than word vomiting everything you know and do, also shows people you care. I was starting to see how I could connect my past experiences with my present and leverage each skill I had learned to propel me forward in my career. Just as in my client work in Principal Connection, all I had to do was shift the focus of the conversation from myself to them and wonderful things started happening again.

When we adopt an "others-centric" approach—focusing on "them," helping "them" connect with resources, supporting "their" dreams, and showing "them" a new path forward—our age, gender, and experience matter little in the interaction. Nobody is concerned about your age or gender when you become the catalyst that determines whether they achieve their aspirations or remain stagnant. Consequently, as a result of learning how to connect with people and add value to their lives, I rapidly developed into a proficient recruiter.

Equipped with these newfound skills and a desire to be as far away from the sinister passenger as much as possible, my career began to accelerate swiftly. Over the years, I have observed that when people encounter significant challenges at home, they typically react in one of two ways: they either let their home issues consume them, affecting their professional life, or they immerse themselves in their work to escape from their personal problems. I chose the latter approach, though I am not saying that either is correct.

I woke up early, arrived at the office ahead of time, and stayed throughout the day. I attended evening drinks, dinners, and engaged in networking. I even worked on Saturday mornings. I did everything imaginable to avoid being at home.

As a result, I earned a promotion to a management position within nine months of arriving in Kansas City. I was tasked with leading a small group of life and disability agents, building my own unit by recruiting both newcomers to the industry and experienced agents. This marked my shift from being a passenger to a guide on this journey. It was my first substantial leadership role in the professional sphere.

As I focused on recruiting, I began to imagine each potential recruit driving their own bus with their own, unique passengers. This perspective guided my approach to recruitment and team-building. Every single agent had a different business model, which meant they needed different people on their bus at any given time to help them reach their desired destination or target market. In other words, who are the people my agent needs to be surrounded by in order to reach the clients he/she/they are trying to acquire? Taking it one step further, who needs to be on the bus to ensure my agent actually places business with those target clients? I loved this puzzle. Who was on their bus? Who should be on their bus? Who's currently on their bus that should probably be coached up or coached out so that my agent has the smoothest ride possible?

Before any of this could happen, I realized that I needed to believe in my agents more than they believed in themselves. By demonstrating my belief in them, their dreams, and the feasibility of their aspirations, I instilled in them my own conviction. I had borrowed others' belief in me to achieve a goal countless times by this point, and this was my chance to begin paying it forward. Individuals with unwavering self-confidence, when paired with the right resources, become unstoppable.

A great manager will equip you with the tools and resources needed to succeed. A great leader will teach you how to leverage tools and resources to generate outcomes. That's it. I was twenty-five when I realized that my ability to network and forge deep, personal connections would take me further in life than any degree or certification ever could.

By the age of 27, my reputation had preceded me in Kansas City. I'll always remember the day my phone rang and a complete stranger introduced herself. "Hello, my name is…" I can't recall her name; let's call her Betty. "My name is Betty. I just relocated to Kansas City, and after asking around for people I should connect with, three individuals recommended you as the person to know. I'm reaching out to see if we could arrange a meeting, as I'm seeking to expand my network here in Kansas City."

I consulted my coach, Breandan, and she responded, "Congratulations! You're what we call a super connector." At that point, there were very few meetings I would turn down. Every interaction taught me something new and often opened doors. Not all doors were worth opening, but I was still young and inexperienced enough that the more people I knew, the broader my network became, providing more opportunities to connect people with resources and steer them away from unfavorable paths.

I relished the opportunity to open people's eyes to new possibilities and connect them with others who could assist them in achieving what had been eluding them. I knew that neither I nor Principal was the right fit for everyone. Maintaining the integrity to inform someone that they would fare better by staying where they are rather than switching to another firm proved to be an uncommon practice in the industry. I never wanted to recruit someone if I wasn't reasonably certain their move would result in their success and the surpassing of their own expectations. Altering someone's livelihood is a significant responsibility. If they faltered due to a decision I influenced, resulting in benefit to me (since my bonuses were tied to my recruiting numbers) but ultimately detrimental to them, causing their business to suffer, then I held myself accountable for the repercussions—unpaid mortgages, credit card debt, job loss. It was a weighty matter.

Not every individual I recruited into the industry succeeded. Nevertheless, they all reported gaining valuable experience, learning something new, and boosting their confidence for their next role. That, to me, constitutes a triumph.

Lessons Learned:

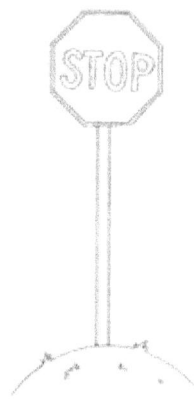

1. *You will never please everyone.*

2. *Focus on what you're doing, not on what you're not doing.*

3. *In business, put others' needs before your own and you will never have anything to regret.*

CHAPTER NINE

There is More than One Way to Travel

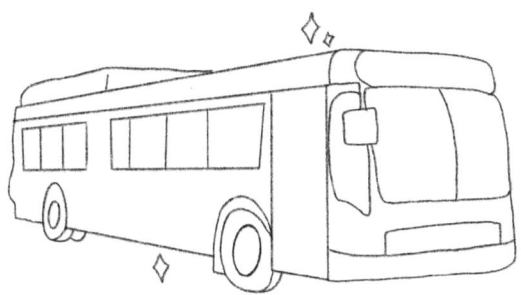

Breandan made a warm introduction for me to an up-and-coming financial advisor at Smith Barney, and I had been calling and trying to get in touch with him. While the wirehouses (Smith Barney, Morgan Stanley, UBS, Merrill Lynch, etc.) had a different business model than Principal, our broker-dealer, Princor, was evolving and expanding. For the right advisor, a move could make sense.

He finally called me back and said, "I really am not interested in having a conversation with you, but I've heard a lot about you around town, and I'd like to introduce you to my Branch Manager, M.A. Mullis."

As I mentioned earlier, there were very few meetings I was unwilling to take. I sat down with M.A. for breakfast one day, unsure where the conversation would go. After some time, she said, "I think you should go through our Manager Assessment and come work for me."

I was floored. All I had heard for the last five years was how terrible wirehouses were. They were the "dark side" of the business. I didn't want to insult her and did not know what to say, so I blurted out the first thing that came to my mind.

"I'm thinking of moving to Chicago."

I was not thinking about moving to Chicago. I had only visited Chicago once while in the third grade.

"That's great!" She replied. "I'd very much like to introduce you to my Regional Director and my Divisional Director up in Chicago."

Unintentionally, I had backed myself into a corner.

Later that afternoon, I got a call from one of the Chicago Director's assistants, Melissa. It was a Thursday, and she said, "I'm reaching out because Doug and Bill would like you to join them for lunch this Monday."

Oh, thank God, I thought. Here's my out. "Oh, gosh, Melissa, thank you so much for the call. I know you probably don't realize this, but I'm not actually in Chicago. I'm in Kansas City."

There was a moment of silence on the other end of the line, followed by, "Yeah, I know. That's why I'm calling. To make your flight arrangements to come up here for lunch this Monday."

Once again, I found myself speechless. I was *really* backed into a corner now. So, I just said, "yes." The next thing I knew, I was getting on an airplane Monday morning and flying to Chicago to have lunch with a Regional Director and Divisional Director of one of the largest wirehouses in the United States of America. I started to feel a little like Jim Carey in the movie *Yes, Man,* where Mr. Carey commits to saying "yes" to every question asked of him.

They sent a car and driver to meet me at the airport. I had seen this in movies, but never in my wildest dreams did I ever imagine my name would appear on a board, held up by a driver in a suit and hat at the bottom of an escalator. Was this really how other people traveled?

When I arrived at the Chicago Mercantile Exchange where Smith Barney had its regional offices, I found out the Divisional Director, Doug, had been called away to an urgent meeting, so it would just be the Regional Director, Bill, and me for lunch.

Bill Lee was the most polished, professional man I had ever laid eyes on. Think of an older Don Draper from Mad Men. I would later learn his nickname was "The Teflon Man" because everything seemed to slide right off him. He was kind with piercing blue eyes and had a voice better suited for radio than board rooms.

As our lunch progressed, I answered his questions and asked many of my own. He seemed to find me amusing. Love it or hate it, one of my qualities is that I am authentically and unapologetically who I am 100 percent of the time. I'm not everyone's cup of tea, so to speak, but I've always strived to surround myself with people who like and want to support me for who I am, not who they *think* I might be. If who I am is not the right fit for a work environment, a relationship, or a volunteer role, then it's not the right fit for either of us. Better to let it go!

"Angela, if you could drive any car, what kind of car would you drive?" he asked, close to the end of our lunch.

I looked him square in the eyes and said, "I would drive an Aston Martin." The only reason I even knew what an Aston Martin was is that I had seen a James Bond film over the weekend.

Little did I know Bill was a huge car aficionado, and he found my answer intriguing. "Really! Which model?" he asked.

Uh oh. I did not know anything about these cars! Building on my years of thinking quickly on my feet, I replied deviously, "Does it really matter?"

"Touché," he said, smiling.

Suffice it to say, the lunch was a success, and I was invited to participate in the Management Assessment at Smith Barney.

Assessment took place about a month later, and there were two other gentlemen—both internal candidates—going through Assessment the same day. It was a very intense process that lasted about eight hours, divided into three different segments. One is an inbox exercise (yes, literally how well you can organize your email inbox), one is a role-play exercise, and the third is a delegation exercise. Everything was timed in some strange interval—17 minutes if memory serves. There were three inbox exercises, three delegation exercises, and three role-plays. 17 minutes to complete each.

It quickly became clear in my inbox and delegation exercises that I had no idea what I was doing. I did not even understand half the words in the exercises because they were either Smith Barney or wirehouse jargon. Who's to say? How was I supposed to know what the urgency was behind a CAES report or whose job it is on your management team to review it? I didn't even know what a CAES report was. I was relieved when someone walked in and handed me my first role-play exercise. Finally, something I'm usually pretty good at.

I had eight minutes to review the scenario and prepare my thoughts and nine minutes to complete the role-play. In my first scenario, I was to meet with a seasoned financial advisor whose revenue had dropped so significantly that he was no longer entitled to two sales assistants and was upset that the firm had reassigned one assistant to another advisor.

As I walked into the room, I held my head high and smiled, my eyes locking with the gentleman sitting at a table, alone, in the center of a U-shaped configuration of evaluators. Ignoring them (mostly because looking at them would make me nervous), I walked right up to the man in the middle of the room, stuck my hand out, and said, "Hi! I'm Angela, the new Assistant Manager here. It's a pleasure to meet you."

He shook my hand and said, "Hello," but not much else. Awkward.

He was a big man, probably twice my size, and seemed to have a chip on his shoulder. I did not know if that was part of the role-play or if he really had an attitude.

"I appreciate you taking the time to meet with me and understand you have some concerns about your coverage."

"You bet your ass I have concerns about my coverage."

Then he just started going off. Everything from what was "being taken away from him," to "how was he expected to run a business without support," to how "management has no idea what they're doing."

I listened to him, a little taken aback. "John, I appreciate your situation. It's clear you care about your clients and want to provide them with the best service possible. I'm here to help you."

"Help me?!" He screamed. "Help ME???" At this point, he got up from his chair and towered over me, pointing his index finger at me aggressively. "What can YOU possibly do to help ME? You just started here. You don't even know the first thing about my business. I heard you came from the insurance industry. What do you even know about capital markets?"

So, this is happening, I thought to myself. I sat there quietly, my hands folded in my lap, taking it all in, and something from my childhood flashed through my mind.

I remember my father coming home from a trip one evening, more tired than usual.

"How was your trip, Dad?" I asked.

"Hard, but successful." He went on to explain that he had sold some banking software to a longtime client, but the implementation had not gone well, and the bank was furious. He had tried everything he could think of to get the course corrected, but the harder he tried, the worse things got. The bottom line was his company had dropped the ball and the client was out for blood.

He got up that morning, put on his suit and tie, and stopped at Fin & Feather, an outdoor retail store, on his way out of town. He picked up a pack of targets—the kind you would use for practice with a bow and arrow. When he arrived at the bank, he got out of his car, took his shirt and tie off, and taped a target to his chest. Then he put his shirt, tie, and jacket back on.

He walked into the bank; the air palpable. "They're waiting for you in the conference room, Dave," the receptionist said.

As he made his way to the conference room, he knew his meeting would not go well.

"Folks, there's no way around it. We screwed up, and you need someone to blame."

He rose from his chair and seemingly began to undress. As he took his jacket off, loosened his tie, and unbuttoned his shirt, faces went white.

"I'm here, and I'm ready. You have ten minutes to take all your best shots. Once you've exhausted your anger and frustration, we'll sit down and, together, figure out how to move forward. Now go! Let me have it!"

The room erupted into laughter as he stood there, a target secured to his chest under his dress shirt.

"Okay, Dave, you've made your point. Let's get to work," the bank President said.

I thought of my dad, standing there at the head of a boardroom, a target taped to his chest. When John stopped yelling at me, I said very calmly, "Are you finished?"

"Yeah," he said, indignantly, sitting back down.

"Do you feel better?" I asked.

He stared at me, untrusting. "A little."

"Good," I replied. "Sometimes we need to just get things off our chests. Now, as for what I know and how I can help. You're right. I do come from an insurance background and don't know a lot about capital markets just yet. But what I do know is how to help people grow their businesses. As I understand it, the way it works around here is that you are allotted coverage based on your production, correct?"

"Yes," he said.

"Great," I replied. "So, presumably, the reason you have lost some coverage is that your production has dropped from where it once was, correct?"

"I guess." He was still indignant.

"John, if you don't mind my asking, what's happening in your life that's causing your production to drop? Because it's clear you care very much about your clients, your business, and your team."

He went on to tell me that he was going through a divorce which was causing him to lose focus and spend more time away from the office than he had anticipated. I listened to him and did my best to empathize with him.

"I'll tell you what," I said. "Let's set some time up later this week to go through your book to see where there may be some low-hanging fruit to generate some business for you. Part of the reason they brought me on board is my expertise in insurance, and as I understand it, dropping insurance tickets is one of the best ways to generate revenue, is it not?"

"It is," he said.

"Are you open to letting me help you?"

"I am," he replied.

"Wonderful! Is Wednesday or Thursday better for you?"

Having gained his commitment, I thanked him for his time, asked if there was anything else I could do for him today, stood up, shook his hand, told him I looked forward to seeing him again Wednesday and walked out of the room. The whole thing took less than 5 minutes. I still had four minutes remaining. Surely, I had done something wrong if I did not use the allotted time.

The firm brought lunch in for all three of us candidates. I sat quietly, listening to the internal gentlemen talk about their role-plays and how they had problem-solved the fictitious Advisor's problem. All I could think to myself was, *I am so out of my depth here. I have no idea what they're talking about. I think I gave all the wrong answers. I was focused on the relationship, not products or solutions. I am definitely failing.* After I had eaten, I snuck off into a corner for a bit of privacy and called a friend.

"I think I've made a huge mistake. I don't know what's going on, what half of these words are, or what they want from me. Maybe I should just leave. There's no way that I'm going to make it."

"Don't leave!" she said. "Stick it out to the end. If you're going down, go down in a blaze of glory!" At least she made me laugh.

The second half of the day was a blur and, in my mind, even worse than the first half, if that's possible. When it was all over, I got called into Bill's office. As we sat down, he said, "Angela, I've been doing this for a very long time, and I've seen hundreds of candidates go through Assessment. You scored in the top three of any candidates I've ever seen come through here. You do need to work on your delegation skills, however." Well, duh. Had I known what any of the items on the delegation list were and the makeup of my management team, I probably would have done a lot better.

I felt like I was back in that computer lab, staring at the screen the day I passed my Series 7. That now familiar rush of nervous excitement coursed through me. I knew nothing about capital markets. I didn't understand how wirehouses worked. I didn't understand supervisory work in the wirehouse world. But none of that mattered. I was good with people. I was good at making people feel seen, heard, and understood. I was resourceful, scrappy, intuitive, and able to think on my feet. I was not intimidated by anyone, but rather approached every situation with curiosity, a desire to learn, understand, and problem solve.

Years later, after we both left the firm, Bill and I gathered with a few other former colleagues, reminiscing about our connection to one another and our time at Smith Barney. "Bill, do you remember our first lunch when you asked me 'If you could drive any car, what would you drive?'" I asked.

His face lit up. "I do!" he responded. "You said an Aston Martin."

Sheepish, I confessed, "I had no idea what an Aston Martin was at the time."

"I knew it!" He declared, like he had just won a bet. "Well played." You never know when words are going to count and where they're going to lead you. Sometimes you just have to read the room and be bold!

Having passed Assessment, I moved on to interviews with two different branches in Chicagoland a month or two later. I was offered the same position—Assistant Branch Office Manager (ABOM, for short)—in Kansas City and Deerfield, an office on the North Shore of Chicago. It was my choice. For personal reasons, I accepted the position in Deerfield. That's when life really began to change, and the bus began to speed up.

At the time Smith Barney hired me, there were approximately 220 managers around the country. I was the 19th woman and the youngest of all 220 at age twenty-eight. I received a two-year guarantee and quadrupled my annual salary overnight. I called my parents to share the incredible news. Not only was this a major accomplishment and opportunity for me, but Chicago was only two and a half hours from home, whereas Kansas City was five.

After they asked me the now obvious question, "What qualifies you to do this job," which was met with my now-standard response, "I don't know, but someone else clearly thinks that I can do it, and I will rise to the occasion," they asked a new and strange question. "Do you need to live in the largest city in the world to be happy?" No, Mom and Dad, I am not moving to Tokyo. I'm just moving to Chicago. It was around this time I started accepting that my parents and I did not see the world the same way. They come from a time and place where you found contentment in stability and predictability. It was their concern *for me*, not their doubt *in me*, that motivated their questions.

All most parents want is to see their children happy and able to build a life of their own. I kept risking the "known" for the "unknown," and at a fairly rapid pace. I'm certain it seemed like I was making rash decisions in my professional life, in part because I had made some very rash decisions in my personal life. In my mind, there was a clear delineation between personal and professional, but that was something only I could see. Yes, my personal life was teetering on disaster, but my professional life was flourishing, offering up opportunities for growth through change. There was a part of me that felt like this new professional opportunity could somehow fix what had gone wrong for me personally. I did not know how, but I was willing to get on the bus and see where it led.

Up to this point, my faith had remained separate from my everyday life and career. I think that's because it is not socially acceptable to bring your faith to work with you every day. However, I had grown in faith and was finding myself relying more and more on God to get me through each day, largely because of the difficulty I was experiencing personally. I had no real plan when I accepted the job at Smith Barney. I still do not have a plan. My only plan then, and my only plan now, is to continue to listen for God's calling and respond in blind faith.

There's this expression, "Get comfortable being uncomfortable." The first time I heard it, I thought, *Yeah, right... that makes no sense. If you're uncomfortable, how can that be comfortable?* By this time in my career, I knew what it meant. I was twenty-eight, but I had already put myself in so many situations in which I never imagined, growing up as a middle-class kid in Iowa, I would be in. Getting comfortable in the uncomfortable simply means that you're not afraid to try something new, or to say "yes" to something because the outcome is unpredictable. It means you're willing to try, you're willing to fail, you're willing to make a fool of yourself in your pursuit of self-actualization.

As my work at Smith Barney began, it was like I had gone from riding a public Greyhound to traveling in style on a luxury bus you see on *Lifestyle of the Rich and Famous*. It only took a few months for me to realize my previous bus had, in fact, been hijacked by the sinister passenger who had systematically downgraded my travel experience. Being on this new bus gave me the confidence and clarity I had been seeking. I did not want that passenger on this new, amazing bus with me, so I sprinted to the front, pulled on the lever to the door as hard as I could, and while the bus was still in motion, kicked my sinister passenger to the curb!

I was traveling in style, and it was marvelous. I loved my coworkers. I loved the advisors I was working with. I loved that no one chewed tobacco at work or ever knocked their cup of spit over on my notepad. I loved that people took pride in their appearance, wore suits to work, drove nice, clean cars, and got manicures (even the men). As the financial world began falling apart in late 2008, we still managed to have fun nearly every day. We supported each other. We relaxed together. It was a community of people who were doing the best we could for our clients and for each other. We did not know what the future held from one day to the next, but we knew we would get through it together.

When the announcement came that Morgan Stanley would be acquiring Smith Barney, it felt more like a forced bus transfer than an upgrade in travel. We actually thought that we were going to be acquiring Wells Fargo at the end of 2008, so imagine our surprise when the bus we were on came to a screeching halt, and all managers were asked to exit the bus and wait on the curb for further instructions. Because the firms were merging, many of the roles we filled were duplicated. We would all have a chance to re-interview for our positions, but about half of us would lose our jobs. The kicker was we weren't the only firm merging. Consolidation was happening everywhere. Sometimes your bus collides with another, and there are only so many seats available on the bus that still runs. You can either start walking and look for a new bus ahead, or you can roll the dice, hoping to get selected for a seat and head blindly in the direction of the surviving vehicle.

I chose to wait and re-interviewed for my job. It was one of the worst days of my life. All the ABOMs from the entire region for both Smith Barney and Morgan Stanley were brought into the Regional Office in downtown Chicago to interview with 3 or 4 different Branch Managers and Regional Managers on the same day at the same time. We all sat in the waiting room together, waiting for our turn to be called to meet individually with the interviewers. Imagine it—people you consider friends and colleagues, all sitting together in one room, competing for the same job. Each interviewer would come to the waiting area, grab one of us for an interview, and then return us to the waiting area for a period of time before the next interview. This went on for several hours until we had all met with each of the interviewers. As the day wore on, the mood got heavier. We all knew that half of us would be losing our jobs by the end of the month. It was like the corporate version of *The Hunger Games*.

In the end, the odds were in my favor. I was offered my same job—ABOM for the North Shore. For me, the cultural differences between Smith Barney and Morgan Stanley were vast. It quickly became evident that Morgan Stanley and I were not a fit. I was in therapy at the time, once a week, working on personal growth. Over time, my sessions with my therapist transitioned to being less about the personal choices I was making in my life and more about my ability to survive in my professional environment. Even though I was still under my original two-year agreement with the firm, I talked to a lot of the people I worked with about wanting to leave and wanting to pursue other opportunities. The transition and the merger were difficult for everyone. Consistency in leadership was something the advisors and staff I worked with craved. In fact, so many people told me that I was the bright spot in their day, that I was what kept them going, that I felt like I owed these people—the passengers on my bus—the respect of staying and trying to make their lives as easy and as good as possible, despite my own misery. I realize now their encouragement was their way of trying to make *me* feel better. No one really needed me. Everyone is replaceable. Even me.

As a strategy to deal with my work-related depression, one of the exercises my therapist suggested was that I write down positive affirmations on index cards and read them out loud to myself every day before walking into the office. Let me tell you, if you reach the point where you're writing down positive affirmations on index cards and reading them out loud to yourself before you walk into the workplace, you're on the wrong bus.

Lessons Learned:

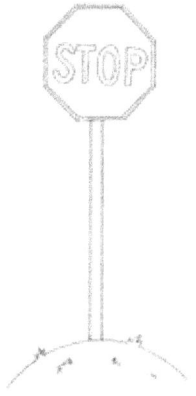

1. *The more people you know, the more opportunities you will have. You don't have to say "yes" to them all, but sometimes saying "yes" can lead to something great.*

2. *Be authentically who you are 100 percent of the time.*

3. *Everyone is replaceable.*

CHAPTER TEN

You Haven't Lived Until You've Been Escorted off the Bus

The surefire way to know you are not only not in the right seat on the bus but that you're on the wrong bus entirely is when the bus stops and other passengers actually escort you off. In early summer 2010, I was RIFed (Reduction in Force), and my employment with Morgan Stanley ended. It was not entirely unexpected. I had been feeling uneasy in the role for some time, and the night before I received a call from a well-meaning wholesaler saying, "I'm really sorry about your job loss."

"What are you talking about?" I asked. Apparently, the plans had been leaked. Walking into the office that morning, I felt somewhat prepared. When it was over and I left the office, I realized I had been staying not because of my two-year agreement, because I wanted the job, or because I was trying to make life better for others, but because I was so afraid of what I would do without it.

I had no idea what else was out there for someone like me. My background was atypical. Would there be another bus willing to let me on? Being forced off the bus, standing there in the middle of the proverbial street with other buses whizzing by me, my fear set in. I was afraid to put myself out there. I was afraid of being rejected. I was afraid of being unemployed and once again pictured my future self, homeless and destitute. I prayed for an answer.

My time at Principal had taught me to be a consummate learner. Not only did the firm invest in professional image and communication training for me, they had also put me through "Integrity Selling" and "Managing Goal Achievement," both by Ron Willingham. As incentives in those courses, facilitators handed out books like *The Richest Man in Babylon*, *Think and Grow Rich*, and *The Secret* to those who made significant strides from one week to the next. As a result, I was indoctrinated early in my career to believe that we get back from the world what we put into it. Give generously and be blessed with abundance.

I wanted my next job to fill me with a sense of purpose and for my work to have greater meaning. With all that fear and uncertainty boiling up inside me, I did the only logical thing I could think to do: I made the single largest gift to charity I had ever made. With $5,000, I fed thousands of children in Africa with food packets malnourished bodies can actually process through a program at my parent's church.

I was unemployed with bills to pay and also had a six-figure legal obligation due to choices I had made in my personal life. But rather than feeling pressure, all I felt was a giant sense of relief. I trusted in God and His infinite plan for my life.

My parents did not share my enthusiasm for unemployment. I felt like they were ashamed I had been let go, and I felt like a disappointment. I was raised with the mentality that you should aspire to work for one company your entire life that has a great pension plan. If you take care of the firm, the firm will take care of you. I wanted that—really, I did. It's why I had pursued employment with Principal with such tenacity and vigor. The fact that I had already had four employers—soon to be five when I got new employment—was incomprehensible to my parents. "You just can't seem to stick to anything," they told me.

The logical, processing side of me tried to walk them through it. "It's not my fault that I keep getting promoted and offered new positions of opportunity. That's also not a bad thing, is it?"

"But even when you get promoted or move up, you're still not satisfied. You need to pick something you can do for the rest of your life and just be good at that." What I could not get them to see was that it had nothing to do with satisfaction. I was satisfied and happy in every role I had up until my time at Morgan Stanley. And let's be honest, that's not a job I pursued, per se. For me, it was always about I CAN: Constant And Neverending Improvement in the pursuit of self-actualization.

The world had changed. Beginning in the early 2000s, gone were the days when employees stayed with one employer forever. Most people my age will have five or more employers over their lifetime of work. Not only that, when you're escorted off a bus, you don't really have an option of staying. You have to look for something new, but that doesn't mean that you have to go back to the job you had before. I was ready to use everything I had learned about myself, the knowledge I acquired, and the skills I had developed to move into a new role that would bring joy, fulfillment, and purpose to my life. Every opportunity I had embraced leading up to this moment gave me the chance to meet different people, learn about different businesses, and explore areas I never even knew existed. With my move to Smith Barney, I had realized there wasn't just one bus company out there, there were millions.

The possibilities—even within my industry—were endless. With experience in insurance-based and capital markets-based wealth management, the world was my oyster.

One of the funny things about being let go from a job is who reaches out to you in the aftermath and who does not. As I've spoken with people in subsequent years who also got let go from their jobs, they all say the same thing. You're always surprised by who calls to say, "Hey, I heard what happened. I'm really sorry. If there's anything I can do to help you as you move forward, please let me know." Then there are people you never hear from who you thought would be the most likely to reach out, often the people you supported the most.

This is the thing about human behavior: it's unpredictable. You cannot rely on others to problem-solve for you, but you can ask for help. And that's exactly what I did.

I reached out to Dan Lengyl, who was with MetLife Investors at the time. I had met Dan during my time at Morgan Stanley, had a great deal of respect for him, and thought he was one of the smartest and most personable people I had ever met. He was kind enough to take my call and give me some advice.

"You know what I would do if I were you?" he asked. "I would take this time to sit down and make a list of everything you're good at—personally and professionally. Then go through that list and cross off everything you don't like. Next, make a list of everything you're not good at. Once that's finished, go through and cross off all the things you're not good at that you don't like. That will leave you a list of things you're good at and like, and things you're not good at, but hope to improve.

"From there," he went on, "Make a new list of the items above and recraft your resume to reflect the skills that match what you are good at and like, and what you aspire to. That will not only help you narrow down the kinds of jobs, firms, and cultures you want to join next but will help you attract the kinds of opportunities that build on your natural skills and abilities."

It was great advice, but let me be fully transparent: I got let go at the beginning of a beautiful Chicago summer and I lived in Wrigleyville. I spent most of my days taking walks, riding my bike along Lake Michigan, and catching up on some much-needed sleep. I had just spent nearly 2 years getting up at 4:00 a.m. every day, driving 28 miles to my gym, working out at 5:00 a.m. so I could shower and be in my North Shore office by 7:30, working until 6:30 at night, then either embarking on my 2-hour drive home down the Edens or attending a work dinner, then embarking on what was still a 2-hour drive home on account of road construction. I was beat!

I took time over the next few weeks to go to the gym, read, work on my Spanish skills (which had regressed significantly since I left Principal Connection in 2005 and no longer spoke the language every day), and binge-watched TV I had never seen. I think I watched the entire first season of *24* in 24 hours.

I also realized that because all I had done since moving to Chicago was work, I did not have any friends—not one—who were not also work colleagues. I began to wonder who from my hometown lived in Chicago. I got on Facebook and searched for people I knew who were living in the city. One of the first people to come up was Peter Rossman. Peter and I had gone to preschool together in Iowa City. After that, he attended the only private Catholic school in town, Regina, and I went to the public schools on the east side of town. Funnily enough, we had double-dated to my junior year Homecoming—him with my friend, Brooke, and me with his friend, Chris, who had transferred from Regina to Iowa City High. That was probably the last time we had spoken.

I reached out anyway with, "Hey, I'm living in Chicago now. Do you want to get together for a drink sometime?"

"Hi! Sure!" he replied, almost immediately. "What are you doing tonight?" It turned out we lived about 10 minutes from each other, and that very night, we got together and caught up like old friends over a beer. I learned that Peter was working for McKenzie Group—a consulting firm—and that he was actively involved with a nonprofit in Chicago called Mercy Home for Boys & Girls. He was so passionate about their work and loved being able to use his skills and enthusiasm to help the organization better serve at-risk youth in Chicago. It sounded very cool.

This is when I realized that, not only did I have no friends, I also had no hobbies. I did not give back to the world in any meaningful way. Peter was working and volunteering, doing something purposeful with his life. I did not know what that would be for me, so I started with just going to Mass every Sunday. That would have to suffice until I found a new job. At that time, I firmly believed that paid employment took precedence over volunteerism. Therefore, my work schedule would dictate my availability for volunteer work. Over time, I would come to see the flaw in my thinking.

"The list" was never far from my mind, so after a few weeks, I sat down with a pad of paper and a pen (a blue pen, of course). What am I good at? This was a very long list at this point. I'm not trying to sound arrogant, but at this point in my life, I was in my early 30s and had broad work experience. I had been in the full-time, professional workforce since I was twenty-one. The most recent jobs I held were ones that people work two decades or more to secure. Not only that, but I had also started as a bank teller—for goodness' sake—when I was sixteen! Most of my coworkers were in their 40s and 50s, even then. So yes, I had a pretty long list of skills I had developed over the last decade and a half that I was pretty darn good at. Building relationships, listening, solving problems, leading teams, foreign languages, building resources, public speaking, writing, and helping people all made it to my list.

As I looked down, I started crossing off items I was good at but did not enjoy. I was really good at recruiting, but I just didn't enjoy it. In fact, I hated it. I was good at creating systems, but it was tedious work for me. I was good at writing, but I hated entering notes about meetings into databases. In fact, I disliked anything having to do with databases or database management, though I certainly saw the value in good, clean data.

Next, I started my list of what I am not good at. Boy, was THAT a long list. After I had exhausted my mind on everything at which I'm terrible—sports of any kind, math, options supervision, reading (I like to read, but I'm a really, really slow reader)—I began crossing off everything I'm not only not good at but don't like. I was left with a list of areas I enjoyed that weren't my strength but in which I wanted to build proficiency. Wealth and estate transfer planning, asset repositioning, and golf.

When I finished my list, I called Dan back. "Dan, I want to thank you. I finished my list, and it was really eye-opening for me." I called it my "Purposeful Work Self-Assessment." You can download a free copy of a guide and begin your own self-discovery by scanning this QR Code.

"I'm happy to hear you took the exercise seriously," he said. "If you don't mind my asking, what's on your list?"

I went through everything with him, and he said, "I think we should talk about a new program we are piloting at MetLife Investors." After several interviews and conversations, I was hired. It was perfect. It exactly matched the list, and the culture was amazing. I was wholesaling life insurance products to financial advisors in wirehouse firms to help their very best clients establish wealth and estate transfer plans utilizing insurance as an asset.

It hit so many of my boxes. I was building relationships with advisors, understanding the needs and wants of their top clients, and finding unique ways to leverage insurance to solve complex wealth and estate transfer planning issues. Having spent the first five years of my career at Principal, I really had a deep understanding of insurance products and the kind of leverage insurance offers that marketable securities simply can't. I loved the idea of uniting my insurance background and capital markets knowledge, the chance to use my relationship building skills to get in front of advisors and their best clients, and the opportunity to present new and fresh ideas to advisors and their clients alike that could change their lives. Most of the clients we worked with had net worths of $5 million and above. We were helping them create plans, ensure a seamless transition of family-owned businesses, and establish legacies for their families. Most excitingly for me, for clients who were charitably inclined, we looked at their overall wealth picture and asked, "How can we reposition some of your assets to offer you greater leverage, more protection in your portfolio, the power to change and save lives when your time on earth ends?"

I loved the work, but my territory left much to be desired. I was living in Chicago, and all of my relationships with financial advisors who trusted me were in Chicago, yet my territory was Wisconsin. I did not have a desire to be away from home for 4 days a week, but I did not have much choice if I was going to succeed. This was, after all, a relationship business.

The training was outstanding, the leadership and people were top-notch, and the resources were best-in-class. I was delighted to learn that Andrew Rinn, a former colleague at Principal, had also made the move to MetLife Investors to be part of their Advanced Solutions team, and I took every opportunity I could to partner with him on seminars and new business. Andrew is brilliant and has taught me more about taxation, wealth transfer, and insurance than any other single person, book, or exam. But something just wasn't clicking. I would later come to realize that sometimes even the most talented people can be set up for failure.

As I began to struggle with meeting my sales goals, Peter and I were spending more time together. Let me be clear—our relationship was strictly platonic. We enjoyed each other's company, and both had flexible work schedules, so grabbing lunch outdoors on a beautiful fall day in Chicago was always a good option. I talked with Peter a lot about what I was doing, what I liked about it, and the struggles I had. One day he asked, "Would you ever consider working for a nonprofit? Mercy Home is looking for a new Director of Planned Giving, and they have been looking for a while."

"Absolutely not." I replied, laughing a bit. I could not imagine leaving my industry or, quite frankly, living on a nonprofit wage. I'd worked too hard to get to where I was. I had my Life and Health license, my Series 7, 9, 10, 24, 63, and 65 licenses (I had clearly mastered the art of standardized testing). I had dedicated a decade of my life to learning everything I could about wealth management. That's where all my connections were. That's where all of my friends were. It would never make sense to leave it all behind to pursue a low-paying job. I mean, God bless. The only reason I was able to meet my six-figure financial obligation even after I lost my job and had been without work for three months was that I worked in an industry that paid really, really well. I couldn't give that up!

"Fair," he said. "Why don't you and your boyfriend come to a charity event we're hosting this weekend anyway? There's someone who will be there I would like to introduce you to. Her name is Cheryl Murphy, Mercy Home's CFO. More than anything, you remind me of each other, and I think you'd make great friends."

"Fair," I replied. A few days later, I attended my very first, Have Mercy! Cheryl was lovely; we enjoyed meeting each other, and life went on.

Then it happened. I came home from a work trip, dropped my briefcase on the floor, left my suitcase in the middle of my kitchen, and kicked off my shoes. Just then, the phone rang. It was my internal wholesaler, Kevin.

"Angela, we had a great day today."

"What do you mean?"

"Well, today you made $25,000."

Tiredly and with a sigh I replied, "That's great, Kevin. Thanks for the call."

I should have been excited. I should have been thinking, *Okay, things are finally starting to come together.* Instead, as I hung up the phone, I just remember feeling tired. As I stood in my kitchen, my gaze was drawn to the corner of my desk in the little area that I used as a den. On the corner of my desk, I saw a letter from Mercy Home for Boys & Girls. It felt like the Holy Spirit was tapping me on the shoulder.

When Peter had asked me whether I would ever consider working for a nonprofit, I dismissed it out of hand and had not given it a second thought in months. But maybe, just maybe, this is what God was calling me to do. I picked up the letter and read it. It was a plea from Fr. Scott Donahue, asking me to decorate a placemat for Thanksgiving dinner for a child living in their home.

I wonder how much the Director of Planned Giving makes. I wonder how much I spend every month. I had not given much thought to my monthly spending since 2008. I did not want to burn Peter's relationships or waste anyone's time at Mercy Home if I could not afford to make the transition. I had already downsized my life and personal belongings following a divorce, and I was not in a place where I felt like I could manage with much less. I liked my lakefront apartment, my car was paid off, and I was working on rebuilding my savings after fulfilling my large legal obligation. I sat down and put pencil to paper and figured out what my actual budget was. Okay, maybe if I could do with fewer shoes, I could actually make this work. Rebuilding my savings would have to wait, but maybe, just maybe, this is what God intends for me.

I thought about my list, and my childhood aspirations of wanting to help people, to give back, and make the world a better place. I was still attending Mass every week, but I wasn't doing anything more to shine God's light and love into the world. I had also become disillusioned by ultra-high-net-worth people and their families. Very few of them were charitably inclined, probably fewer than five percent of those I had worked with. It seemed they were only interested in protecting their wealth and passing it on to their children and grandchildren. While I believe there are many reasons for this, I still found it depressing. When a sale went through for me, by and large, all I had accomplished was making wealthy people wealthier. I had not created anything or affected any positive change in the world.

I picked up the phone and dialed Cheryl's number. "Is the Director of Planned Giving still open?"

She was excited to hear from me. "Oh, my gosh, yes! We're still looking for someone. You'd be amazing."

"Whoa," I said. "I'm not there yet, but I'm interested in learning more." That's how my interview process with Mercy Home for Boys & Girls began.

Six months, multiple interviews, and many prayers later, I accepted the position, riding the wealth management bus into the terminal. When I called my boss, Dan, to submit my formal resignation, I could tell he was driving. "Dan, I need to talk to you about something. I can tell you're driving. Could you pull over to the side of the road?"

Annoyed but curious, he did.

"Dan, it may not come as a surprise to you that I'm leaving MetLife."

"I know you've been struggling in the role. What are you planning to do?"

"I have," I said. "I wanted you to pull over because I need to tell you I'm leaving the industry and going to work for a nonprofit." Silence.

"Hello?" I said.

"I'm really glad you told me to pull over," he replied.

I was taking a 66 percent pay cut and had no idea if I was going to like the job enough to make up for what I was leaving behind. What I couldn't confirm at the time, but what I suspected to be true, is that what had made me successful in the corporate world would also make me successful in the nonprofit world. I cared more about helping others accomplish their goals than I did about myself.

Lessons Learned:

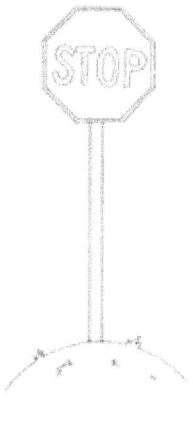

1. It's a good idea to periodically ask yourself: am I staying on this bus because I love it and it is headed to my desired destination, or because I am afraid of getting off?

2. You cannot rely on others to problem-solve for you, but you can ask for help.

3. Sometimes even the most talented people can be set up for failure.

CHAPTER ELEVEN

The New Bus Company

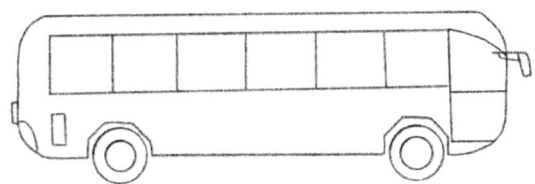

This time, when I picked up the phone to share the news with my parents, their reaction was different. "We cannot think of a better job for you." I don't think they ever saw me as the corporate type. They knew I had a big heart and were relieved when I found a role that allowed me to incorporate my faith and my passion for service into my daily work.

That said, my wealth management industry friends and other family members thought I was crazy. How could I just throw everything away for which I had worked so hard? My licenses. My connections. My industry knowledge. People even offered to help me secure employment at another firm so I "did not have to go work nonprofit." They did not know that, despite my early career success, deep down, I felt incomplete. They did not see the connection between what I had been doing and what I would be doing. They did not know this was my wake-up call to get off the caterpillar pillar.

What's the caterpillar pillar, you ask? When my friend, Brooke Patterson, and I graduated from high school, she gave me the book *Hope for the Flowers*. It's a children's book written for adults. It's about a caterpillar named Stripe. Stripe is born a normal caterpillar, enjoying grass, dirt, and tiny bugs. Then one day, he sees other "crawlers" like him ahead, quickly making their way to some destination in the distance. He follows them, arriving at a giant column made of caterpillars climbing high toward the sky. "What's at the top?" Stripe asks. No one has the answer, leading everyone to believe there's something magical awaiting them at the summit. Because everyone else is climbing, he begins his climb, too. Stripe doesn't make it to the top on his first or even second attempt. But he returns a third time, something inside him dissatisfied, and becomes laser focused on his goal. When he finally reaches the top he hears another caterpillar whisper, "There's nothing here at all." Then another replies, "Quiet, Fool! They'll hear you down the pillar. We're where they want to get. That's what's here."

On his first attempt up the pillar, Stripe met another caterpillar, Yellow. They had come down from the pillar together, romped in the grass, and loved each other. When Stripe decides to tackle the pillar for a third time, Yellow moves on and comes across an old, gray caterpillar, hanging upside down from a branch, seemingly caught in a web. When Yellow offers to help him, he explains he is becoming a butterfly. "It's what you are meant to become," the older caterpillar explains. Yellow could not fathom there is a butterfly inside of her. She asks the old caterpillar, "How does one become a butterfly?"

"You must want to fly so much that you are willing to give up being a caterpillar."

I had spent a decade climbing a pillar. There was nothing at the top that meant anything to me. There was a lifetime of hard work, early mornings, late-night dinners, work travel, entertaining people whose lives were more focused on what they could get, rather than what they could give, and money. But could all the money in the world be worth it if I didn't have time to give back in a way that was meaningful to me? If I didn't have time to forge deep, meaningful relationships? If I didn't give myself the chance to discover who I could become if I made different choices? I wanted to fly so much that I was willing to give up who I was.

I wasn't happy. It wasn't like I had aspired to a career in wealth management. It was simply the conduit that allowed me to put into practice what I had aspired to all those years ago: public speaking, persuasion, and foreign language. If you're going to speak in public, you have to speak about something, and the chance to learn about investments and insurance—something I could apply to my own life—seemed like a good choice. The rest of my career, the road I had taken, was just one bus transfer after another, building on the skills learned in one job and parlaying them to the next. None of it was a conscious choice after that first job as a Benefits Service Representative. It was like I had gotten on a bus line that had a massive fleet of buses from which to choose, but they were all circling at the same destination.

Like many people, I never believed work was supposed to fill you with joy and satisfaction. I viewed it as a means to an end. I thought you selected a profession in which you could make a decent living, do that for 40-45 years, and when you retired, THAT was when it was acceptable to do something more altruistic, more meaningful with your life. It's the adult, responsible thing to do: work to earn a living, provide for your family, and when you retire, then, and only then can you travel, give back through volunteerism, hone your golf game, or maybe even learn something new, like how to play the ukulele.

Little did I know there were other bus companies out there that allowed you to do both: earn a living *and* give back, play golf, travel, and learn new skills. Until now, it was incomprehensible that it was as simple as riding the wealth management bus to the terminal, gathering my belongings (my skills and knowledge), exiting the bus, making the short walk across the bus terminal to where another bus line was housed, and hopping on a different bus that was part of a different line, headed in a different direction.

I fully admit that my imposter syndrome was definitely rearing its angry head. "Imposter Syndrome" is defined as 'the persistent inability to believe that one's success is deserved or has been legitimately achieved as a result of one's efforts or skills.'" That voice of self-doubt was definitely creeping up on me, and more than once, I wondered if I was really making this change because I had been successful and wanted to see what I could become if I had the courage to make a bold move, or because I was a total and complete failure in the corporate world and had no choice but to go in a different direction.

Maybe my skin wasn't tough enough, maybe I wasn't a good enough salesperson, maybe I wasn't a good enough manager, maybe I wasn't good enough at "managing up" to really excel in corporate. When you are in the moment, you will never be able to tell what is true about yourself and what is not. It is only with the benefit of hindsight that you can look back and say, "No, I could not hack it, good thing I made a different choice," or "Yes, I could hack it. I was good. I just was not set up for success," or "I was simply not fulfilled." Years later I would learn that no one in my MetLife Investors cohort succeeded and the division was shut down. It was the model that did not work, not my skills or abilities.

As I began my work at Mercy Home for Boys & Girls, the opportunity to connect people and their money with mission allowed me to gain congruence in my life. I learned about the concept of congruence in the *Managing Goal Achievement* course, by Ron Willingham while at Principal. The "Goal-Achievement Congruence Model" posits there are five different dimensions that must be in harmony, or congruence, if your goals are to be achieved:

1. Goal Clarity
2. View of possibilities
3. Values
4. Achievement Drive
5. Supportive Environment

You can think of each of these as its own circle, one after the other in a row. When they reach congruence, they come together to form one circle. Ron's program is all about singular goal achievement—like growing your business by 20 percent. I had used the model for over a decade to coach the insurance agents and financial advisors I worked with to scale and grow their businesses.

For me, the model had evolved into one with just three circles: core values and beliefs, work, and goals. At the intersection of all three, as in a Venn diagram, was success and fulfillment.

I had a solid, working knowledge of capital markets and a vast knowledge of asset protection products. I knew more than most estate planning attorneys about taxation and asset repositioning. In fact, my passion and love for taxation and asset repositioning still thrives. I read *Trust and Estates* magazine regularly. I hang out with tax attorneys. I have standing quarterly calls with attorneys and CPAs whom I admire and respect, just to get their take on what's happening within our current tax environment, and to see what interesting solutions they are talking about with their best clients.

What I have learned is that every time there's a new bill or a change to the tax code, there is likely a giving and legacy opportunity created for those who are interested in making a lasting impact on their family and/or their community. Another attractive aspect of transitioning into the nonprofit sector was that I no longer had skin in the game. I was paid a salary by the agency—not a commission based on how much I sold. If you ever come across a fundraiser who is making a percentage of what he/she/they raises, RUN! While not illegal, it is against the Ethical Code of Conduct in the nonprofit industry.

Sales, or in this case, donation amounts, did not change my livelihood in any way. I have a friend in philanthropy who always says, "They're just commas and zeroes." A sacrificial gift for one person may be $2,000. A sacrificial gift for another may be $2,000,000. And we get to treat both donors exactly the same. In the fundraising business, every dollar counts. Every dollar has the power to change or save a life.

Whenever I speak to groups of fundraisers, I start by telling them the same thing: "You have the greatest job in the world. You get paid by your agency for the privilege of sitting down with people, listening to their life stories, understanding why they care about your mission and the other nonprofits they support, how they accumulated their wealth, what's important to them, and how they want to have changed the world when their time on earth is over."

What's funny is the same holds true for wealth managers. And where fundraisers and wealth managers alike go wrong is they focus 95 percent of their attention on themselves, their product, or their mission, rather than the client or donor. That is the number one reason wealth advisors fail to grow their businesses and fundraisers fail to meet their goals.

People are fascinating. Their motivations, what they've been through, how they arrived where they are today, what they still hope to achieve and why, are stories that can captivate you far more than any movie or book ever could. Clients and donors (who, by the way, are the same people) just want to be heard. There's an expression in philanthropy: "Listen your way into the gift." In both wealth management and fundraising, 95-98 percent of the sale is active listening; only 3-5 percent is asking. That's because both wealth management and fundraising are asset-raising businesses. They just have different objectives and tax statuses.

It is truly a privilege to listen, objectively, without judgment. It does not matter to me if, at the end of the day, people want to leave 99 percent of their estate to their children and only 1 percent to charity, or they want to leave 99 percent to charity and only 1 percent to their children. People's choices and motivations have nothing to do with me. I am simply the conduit.

For the first time in my life, it was truly just about *them*, about helping them accomplish their goals in the most tax efficient way possible. I quickly noticed that people were more open with me as a gift officer than they were as a wholesaler or financial advisor. I had nothing personal to gain with their decisions, and it made them more comfortable sharing their entire lives with me. I did, however, feel like I had an uphill battle ahead of me.

Up until this point, I had met people through their connection to wealth management firms. I had been talking to people about their money and about their death since I was twenty-three years old. Whenever anyone says, "Isn't fundraising hard?" I always reply, "You think fundraising is hard? Try selling life insurance for a living!"

At Mercy Home, I was meeting people through their connection to the organization. Being of the general opinion that no one is obligated to fund nonprofit work and that most of the extremely wealthy people I had met prior to this were not overly charitably inclined, the knowledge that I needed to raise $15 million a year in order to meet my portion of the $32 million a year budget at Mercy Home was daunting. My reticence was further fueled when I learned the average gift made to the organization was just $24.

Are there enough of those people connected to this organization for me to meet my goal? In the back of my mind, I had a safety net. If I either hated the work or couldn't do it, I could always pull the cord and go back to the wealth management bus line. That's what we need to remember about our lives and our careers. Just because you make a choice today doesn't mean that you can't make a different choice tomorrow. I had two years until my licenses expired. That gave me two years to decide if philanthropy was going to be my path moving forward or if the lower income and the work wasn't for me. Knowing that, I had nothing to lose. There is always a bus to take you back.

As it turns out, the ability to connect people's money with mission was the most gratifying work I could possibly be doing. I loved talking to people about their goals and their objectives, about how they accumulated their wealth, what they've spent their money on in the past, how they felt about it after the purchase or investment, and what other charities they gave to besides Mercy Home.

The benefit was that when I was able to help a donor make a really big gift, that gift went toward helping at-risk youth in Chicago find a home, safety, love, and acceptance, and get an education to break out of the negative cycles of poverty and abuse in which they were born. I loved it so much that I started to get in a little bit of trouble with my boss and mentor, Mimi LeClair.

When it comes to big-dollar gifts, most charitable organizations—universities, museums, theaters, social service nonprofits, etc.—have two departments: Major Gifts and Planned Gifts. Major Gift fundraisers work with donors to make a gift of cash, today. They are immediate gifts. Planned Giving fundraisers cultivate relationships with donors to raise money for future gifts. That includes gifts of appreciated securities, gifts from donor-advised funds, and gifts from IRAs—all gifts that can take 2 days or more before they are received by the nonprofit. It also includes a gift to be received far into the future, like a percentage of someone's estate through a will, a trust, a beneficiary designation, or the residuum of a charitable gift annuity when they ultimately pass. I was hired as the Director of Planned Giving, but because of my wealth management background, I didn't view cash any differently than I did securities, retirement assets, insurance, or personal property. It's all part of someone's net worth with different tax classifications and purposes.

When I sit down with a donor, I want to understand their objectives and goals, first and foremost for their families, and secondly, for the charities about which they care. I was doing a great job cultivating planned gifts and securing new planned giving commitments, which is what I was supposed to be doing, but I was also raising a bunch of money in major gifts - cash gifts now. I met with Mimi every two weeks and every two weeks she would say, "Angie, you're doing a really great job with planned giving, but you have to stay in your lane. Susan and Bradford are our Major Gift officers. You are not a Major Gift officer. You need to refer the cash gifts to them."

I'm one of those people who would rather ask for forgiveness rather than permission. So, every two weeks, I nodded my head and said, "Absolutely, I completely understand," and would go about my business, treating people and their money as one whole picture, rather than a bifurcation made up by the philanthropy sector.

Recruiting, wealth management, and philanthropy are all about relationships. Good recruiters look at every aspect of a recruit's life—their book of business, their team, their goals, and their deficits—to determine whether a move to their firm is a good fit. Great wealth managers look at every aspect of a client's life—their investments, protection products, and asset structure—to make their total assets work smarter. Exceptional philanthropic advisors consider someone's entire net worth, goals, and objectives before asking for a gift. Interestingly, only 3-5 percent of most people's total net worth is held in cash. If you ask most people what their largest asset is, they will say their home or some other tangible property, followed by their retirement account.

It makes absolutely no sense for me to develop a deep, meaningful connection and relationship with a donor and, if in the discovery process we determine that what makes the most sense for them at the time is a gift of cash, for me to turn to them and say, "Mr. and Mrs. Donor, let me introduce you to my colleague who can accept your gift of cash." I refused to do it. Over time, I explained this to my boss using the power of story. When I returned from a donor visit, before I could be chastised for coming back with a check, I would share the story of our conversation with her. In the end, Mimi made the very wise decision to consolidate the Planned and Major Gift departments into one Philanthropy department.

Today, Mercy Home for Boys & Girls, is still one of the only nonprofits in the United States of America that has an integrated philanthropy department where Philanthropic Advisors work with donors, considering their entire financial picture. If your donor doesn't view the money in their brokerage account any differently than the funds in their money market, why should you?

Not everyone at Mercy Home liked the idea of unifying the departments, and we had a bit of a transition. I sat down and gave some serious thought about who should be on the bus with me as I was building out this new model. What kinds of people would make great hires? What seats should they sit in?

I was so blessed to have a number of candidates come our way. Few of them had traditional fundraising backgrounds or estate planning knowledge in their back pocket. But what they all had in common is that, like me, they cared deeply about people. That's what counts. I can teach anyone about taxation and asset repositioning, but I cannot teach someone to genuinely care about and for others. For the first time in my life, I was finding fulfillment and happiness in my work in a way I never had before. I was able to be exceptional without roadblocks, challenges, or bureaucracy.

I was using all of the gifts God gave me to inspire others to give and, in giving, change and save lives. I was inspiring my team, which totaled 20 people between Philanthropic Advisory and Donor Stewardship, to reach their potential. Not only that, but because I was part of such a high-functioning team, I no longer worked 80-hour weeks. This is one advantage of working for a large, high-functioning organization. At smaller nonprofits, people work 60–80-hour weeks because they are stretched for resources. There is often more room for balance at larger organizations.

I had also stopped commuting more than two and a half hours a day. With 52.5 extra hours in every week, I had an opportunity to shine my light a little bit brighter. It was time for me to start giving back.

People always say you get more out of volunteering than you give, and I quickly learned they are right. Regardless of whether you believe in God, the universe, or a higher power, when you spend more time thinking about others than you do thinking about yourself, you find yourself happier and more content with your own life.

My first volunteer role was at Mercy Home for Boys & Girls tutoring one young man, one day a week, after school and dinner. It was simple. Our offices were on the boy's campus and on Mondays, I just stayed late at work and walked across the hall to the home he lived in. I tutored the same young man for three years until he graduated from high school and moved out.

I was nervous at first. It had been a long time since I had been in high school and, while confident in my English and Spanish skills, I doubted my ability to help him in math and science. My Mercy Home coworkers who trained me put my mind at ease. "Angela, it's less about your ability to help him in school and more about just showing up for him."

"What do you mean?" I asked, puzzled.

"Don't be surprised if, for the first few weeks or months, he doesn't even talk to you. Don't be surprised if he puts his head down on the table and refuses to look at you. All these kids know is being let down. They have been let down time and time again, and they have learned how to push people away before they can be let down one more time. Just keep showing up, week after week, and once he learns you're not like everyone else in his life, he'll come around."

That's what I did. I showed up, week after week. Within a few weeks, we were doing great, working together, and his confidence and grades were coming up. Khan Academy helped me with math, and fortunately, he did not need help in science. After about six months, I showed up one night and it was like he was a totally different kid. Disrespectful, rude, and would not try. I stayed my full hour but made no progress. I stopped by the staff office on my way out to ask if something had happened to him. They just laughed.

"The honeymoon phase is over. He's testing you now to see if you'll continue to show up for him, even when he acts out."

"You mean he's doing it on purpose?" I was shocked. I thought we had a good thing going.

"Not consciously," they told me. "Kids who have experienced trauma are used to people trying to help them, but when they make a mistake, that person usually throws their hands up in the air and says, 'If you're not going to help yourself, there's nothing I can do.' Just keep showing up."

I showed up the next week, and he refused to come out of his room. I showed up the following week, and he came out of his room but sat on the couch, a hoodie pulled up over his head and refused to speak with me. We sat there in silence for an hour.

I showed up the next week, and he met me at the table we usually sat at, before all this began, with a bright smile on his face.

"Hi!" he said.

"Hi!" I replied. "Are you ready to do some homework today?"

"Let me ask you something first."

"What's that?" I asked.

"Why'd you keep coming the last few weeks?"

"Because I believe in you."

"Wow," he said. "Okay. Thanks for believing in me. Want to see my homework?"

And that was that. If you take nothing else away from this book, take this: Show Up. With your friends, your children, your spouse, in your work—all you really need to do is show up. It's great if you're prepared and knowledgeable as well, but what people really respect about you is your commitment to do what you say you will do when you say you will do it. If you are not prepared for a meeting, show up anyway and be honest. "I was unable to fully complete [your to-do] by our deadline. It will be ready [future date you will be finished with your task], but I am here because I made a commitment and you/this work are important to me." If you did not get those goodies made for your child's school activity, show up and donate some money. Being present is 90 percent of succeeding.

I loved this volunteer work because I was getting to know our youth better. My student was no different than any other student there. My time with him helped me be a better gift officer. It helped me tell the stories better. It helped me share what the impact was with the donors. It also helped the youth begin to believe in adults again. I had chosen Monday as my tutoring day so I could travel out on donor visits Tuesday-Friday. When I would return, I would share stories about the people who gave money to our organization so that my student, and others, could live there, go to school, and get the help they needed. They LOVED hearing about our donors and seeing pictures of them.

It helped me connect with my coworkers. Regardless of your chosen field of endeavor, when you branch out and spend some time with people in other departments or areas, it helps you do your job better. You understand the inner workings of the organization more than you could otherwise, and it helps you problem-solve when issues arise. This goes back to networking: the more people you know, the more resourceful you can be.

Once the young man I had been tutoring graduated, I was ready to take on some bigger volunteer work. I had been working hard on myself, recovering from the years the sinister passenger had been controlling my bus. As I reflected on those years, I remembered feeling so alone and isolated. Sure, it had been good for my career, but I wished I had had the courage to seek support from someone else. Since I could not go back in time, the next best thing was to be there for someone else.

I did some research on different domestic violence programs in Chicago that needed volunteers. Most of the programs I found required volunteers to work during regular business hours, and while I had some control over my schedule, I was still required to be in the office a minimum of 8 hours a day when I was not on a donor visit trip.

One of the agencies I found, Mujeres Latinas en Acción, had a program for victims of domestic violence, but they also had a program for survivors of sexual abuse. Being a medical and legal advocate for victims of sexual assault meant being on call with three area hospitals for one week a month from 5:00 p.m.-9:00 a.m. and 24 hours on the weekend. When someone came into one of those three hospitals to report a sexual assault, the nurse would ask if they wanted an advocate to be there with them to help explain their options, and their medical and legal rights as it related to their assault.

When you experience the trauma of an assault, your brain sort of shuts down. There's so much information to process for those who seek help: decisions about what to be tested for, what medical options and preventative treatments are available, what legal recourse a survivor might have, whether to file a police report – all of those decisions are exceptionally overwhelming for someone who has just experienced something awful. In fact, for most victims, it's nearly impossible to make sound decisions alone. Medical and legal advocates help explain the options to the survivor and support their decisions, manage the hospital staff to give survivors time to process, and manage police officers who, sadly, are often more interested in not having to fill out a report than taking a survivor's statement.

I decided this was something I wanted to do and something I would be good at. I signed up and dove right into the 40-hour training. What I knew about myself was that my emotional IQ is relatively low, but my intellectual IQ is relatively high. That combination makes me a near-perfect match for difficult work like this. I am good with people, at problem-solving, and calm in a crisis. Because my emotional IQ is on the lower side, I am able to compartmentalize and not absorb the trauma of survivors or let it affect me personally.

During my on-call weeks, my phone rang at least twice a week in the middle of the night. I got out of bed, brushed my teeth, threw my hair in a ponytail, put on some warm clothes, and made my way out into the cold Chicago night, usually between midnight and 3:00 a.m. The hospitals were in some of the worst neighborhoods in Chicago, and while there was usually a police officer or guard to walk me back to my car at the end of the call, there was no one to escort me safely in. The most calls I ever took was 7 in one weekend. I do not remember every survivor I met, though I do recall that only one was over the age of 18. Most calls lasted between 3-5 hours. Some more, if we had to wait for a private room to become available (in Illinois, victims of sex crimes are legally entitled to a private room). I once waited in a boardroom with a victim for 6 hours before a room became available and her rape kit could begin. That was a long night.

It was interesting to hear the reactions from friends and family when I told them about my new volunteer work. I remember my mom telling me that she shared with one of her oldest friends what I was doing, and her friend asked, "Why would anyone ever want to do that?"

"I don't know," my mom replied. "But I think of it like this: Imagine the worst day of your life. Something truly, truly horrendous happens. Who would you want in your corner?"

"You make an excellent point," her friend responded. "But I still don't know why anyone would want to do that."

I was accused of being heartless because of my ability to spend hours with a survivor and their family during the most horrific moment of their lives, then pass them off to the team at Mujeres Latinas en Acción and return to my day-to-day life as though nothing had happened.

I'm not heartless. I don't think heartless people choose to spend their free time giving back like that. I think God blesses us with unique gifts so that we can be His light in the darkness. Some gifts are not as socially acceptable as others. The fact that I am not, by nature, an emotional person isn't always socially acceptable. "You have no feelings," countless people close to me have told me over the years. It is true that I may not experience the range of emotions other people do on a daily basis, but that gift enables me to do work that others simply cannot. I cannot tell you that I *enjoyed* the year I spent before moving from Chicago to Houston, volunteering as a medical and legal advocate, but I can definitively say that being there for people in what's arguably the worst moment of their lives and making that moment even a fraction easier enriched my soul.

Never underestimate the power of your presence and the power of words. Show up. We are programmed to believe that being busy equals being successful. The less time we have, the more important we are. The more important we are, the more protective we need to be of sharing our gifts with others. Not true. It doesn't take much to drastically change the course of someone else's life. I'm not suggesting that everyone has the capacity, or should, go through a 40-hour training and be on call one week a month from 5:00 pm - 9:00 am and 24 hours on the weekend, volunteering as a medical and legal advocate for victims of sexual assault. That would be absurd.

The most impactful part of the work I did was saying to a survivor, "You are strong, you are brave, you survived." It was about listening to them, supporting them, holding their hand (with permission) throughout the exam, making them laugh (when appropriate), or offering a sincere compliment. The greatest impact of all was simply being there. These are free gifts we all have to offer that do not need to take much time.

When Tim McGraw came out with the song "Humble and Kind," I immediately downloaded it. I love the whole song, but I especially love the last stanza:

"When you get where you're going, don't forget—turn back around and help the next one in line. Always stay humble and kind."

That's what this volunteer work was for me. I got to where I was going—I had survived something traumatic in my personal life, and it was time to turn around and help the next one in line. It was time for me to start becoming aware of people in my community who needed help I was uniquely gifted to offer.

Be aware of the people around you. Be present. We live in an age where everyone seems consumed by their own lives, by social media, and by their phones. (I truly think I'm the only person out there who isn't looking at my phone while driving.) Look up! A kind word, a hug, a sincere compliment, or even just a smile can be the fuel someone you don't even know needs to not give up.

Everything seemed to be hitting on all cylinders. I loved my work, I had the right people in the right seat on the bus, my values, beliefs, and goals were working synergistically together, and I was finally in a wonderful, supportive, loving relationship in my personal life. However, any time things get really, really good in life, they seem to be short-lived. Within a year of all these blessings, my exceptional partner got a job offer for his dream job in Houston, TX. As much as I loved him, I did not want to move to Houston.

"You can't move to Houston!" Friends and family told me. "You have worked so hard to get to where you are. You're finally happy. You can't give all that up."

There it was again. "Giving it all up." But what would I be giving up, really? By this time in my life, I had come to view all new experiences as good experiences. When you learn something new—about yourself, about your relationships, about the world—you know more than you did before and are better positioned to make informed decisions moving forward.

With that in mind, I decided it would be far easier to find a new job than a new partner, so I went to Mimi, resignation letter in hand. It's true what they say, "We make plans, and God laughs," because God always has a plan greater than our immediate wants and needs. What I didn't know was that same day, one of our best, strongest fundraisers at Mercy Home had also resigned, and the agency couldn't afford to lose both of us at the same time. It was 2014, and in the entire 127-year history of Mercy Home for Boys & Girls, there had never been a single remote worker. But there is an exception to every rule, and this time, I was the exception. I was offered the opportunity to continue to work for Mercy Home remotely from Houston and continue to manage my team as long as I continued to fundraise and meet the annual budget.

On July 1, 2014, we packed up our condo and my two cats and relocated to Houston.

Lessons Learned:

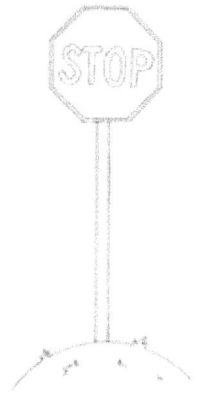

1. *"You must want to fly so much that you are willing to give up being a caterpillar."*

2. *Just because you make a choice today doesn't mean that you can't make a different choice tomorrow.*

3. *Show Up.*

CHAPTER TWELVE

Starting My Own Bus Line

From Forbes.com: "According to the Small Business Administration (SBA) Office of Advocacy's 2018 Frequently Asked Questions… only about half of small businesses survive past the five-year mark, ranging from 45.4 percent to 51 percent, depending on the year the business was started." This begs the question: If you have stable employment with great benefits, working in a job that brings you personal joy and satisfaction, why would you leave to start your own small business (bus line)?

To understand the thought process, you must first understand the situation. If I had one piece of advice to offer about moving to Houston, Texas, it is to not do it on July 1. July and August are the absolute hottest months of the year, and I booked my first trip back to Chicago as soon as I could. The relief I felt as I walked through O'Hare to catch the blue line down to Mercy Home was like a welcome blanket, covering me in the comfort of home. Grateful for the opportunity to maintain my relationships and keep my job, I was determined to make sure no one thought I was missing a beat. I spent two weeks a month in Chicago, a week in Houston, and a week somewhere else in the country, visiting donors. In fact, in the first three years I lived in Houston, I never spent more than three consecutive nights at any one single address. I was always on the go, working, raising money, and trying to spend as little time as possible in Houston.

I despised Houston for a number of reasons aside from the heat, but all that changed while standing in line in boarding group two at George Bush Intercontinental Airport at 5:00 am on a Monday, on my way back to Chicago. We all know the adage: "She's never met a stranger," and that is certainly how most people would describe me. My husband calls me "the friend of the friendless." I had been Houston-based for a little over a year, and part of my dislike for the city was my lack of connection to it. With my demanding travel schedule, I didn't have many friends or much purpose in my community. On this particular morning, however, standing in line next to me was a beautiful, tall, sophisticated woman wearing a gorgeous pashmina scarf. I said to her, "Wow, what a lovely pashmina."

"Oh, thank you so much," she said brightly. "I just bought it this weekend." The conversation took off, and as sleepy travelers looked at us with daggers in their eyes for our early morning peppiness, I learned she was from Houston, had moved away for a while, and had just returned home. As we were talking, I thought, *If I'm ever going to make Houston my home, I need to make friends like this.* Nervous but determined, I gave myself an internal pep talk. *You can do this.* Remember how easy it was to make friends in kindergarten? We didn't have any inhibitions back then; we weren't self-conscious. There was no fear of rejection when we walked up to another child and said, "Hi, I'm Angela. Do you want to be my friend?"

I tapped into my inner kindergartner, and as we boarded the plane, I handed her my business card. "Listen, this may sound a little bit strange, but I really don't have any friends in Houston yet, and I would love it if you wanted to be my friend."

"Oh, my gosh!" She said excitedly. "I would love to be your friend! When do you get back?"

"Thursday."

"Great. I'll call you. We'll get together and have drinks." To this day, Traci is one of my dearest friends. She was my second airplane friend, and as I continued to travel, I made many more airplane friends.

Today, about half of my network of friends and acquaintances in Houston stem from people I met on airplanes or in airports. How is this relevant to the story? As adults, we spend way too much time "adulting." Somewhere along the line, we lose the wonder, curiosity, and bravery we had as children. We decide we have enough friends or enough contacts in our lives; we don't need any more. However, if you seek to expand your horizons, to maximize the vast array of opportunities the world has to offer you in your life and through your work, doesn't it naturally follow that having the largest network of people from varied and diverse backgrounds would give you the greatest chance of succeeding? That way, no matter what bus you decide you want to be on, you have a resource to help guide you.

Your community is wherever you are, not where you live or where you grew up. Your community can be anywhere. Best of all, the people you meet along the way, by and large, want to help you! For most of us, it's in our nature. When we help other people, we feel valued. Our skills, talents, and abilities have positioned us to be able to assist someone else in reaching one of their goals. It is the most flattering feeling in the world when someone calls and says, "I'm reaching out because I hope you can help me," because not only is someone seeing us as valuable, but it's a way for us to give back without exerting much effort.

Speaking of giving back, as I settled into my new travel schedule and life in Houston, the itch to give back struck again. Because I was traveling so much, I decided that it was probably not the right time in my life to re-certify with another 40-hour training as a medical and legal advocate for survivors of sexual assault in Texas (each state has a different certification program).

The thing about giving back is that it's addictive. Seeing firsthand the difference I had made in the life of a child by tutoring just one hour a week at Mercy Home and the strength I gave survivors of sexual assault simply by being there and giving them space to make life-altering decisions gave me confidence in my ability to transform the world through more than money. Once you start putting others before yourself, you realize that not only are your problems manageable, but that you have the power within you to forever change the course of someone else's life.

I saw an ad on social media that Big Brothers Big Sisters (BBBS) of Houston was launching a new program called "Mentor 2.0." The program matched mentors with juniors in high school, and the commitment was three years: junior and senior year of high school and year one of college or post-secondary options. Many kids from vulnerable communities do not go on to post-secondary education following high school, or fail in their first year of college because they do not have a support system of people who have completed a post-secondary option themselves or believe in the value of higher education. The idea behind this program was to help provide at-risk youth with that support system; or at least a fraction of a support system.

Being the youngest in my family and never having babysat, I'm not good with little kids. I am, however, great with teens, especially teens who have been forced to grow up too quickly. Most of the communication with Littles was through an app, which I could access from anywhere, and all in-person activities were scheduled far in advance, so I could plan my travel schedule accordingly. I applied and was selected for a screening interview that lasted nearly 3 hours.

I was surprised by many of the questions. The questions were written to determine the motivation of the prospective volunteer. When given a chance to ask questions of my own, I learned the two biggest obstacles BBBS faced were:

1. Having enough men volunteers to match with male Littles. There are typically 100+ boys waiting for a mentor, whereas there is a waiting list of women mentors because women volunteer at a much higher rate than men.

2. People volunteer to be Bigs simply so they can put it on their resume; they do not fulfill the program requirements. In other words, they don't show up for a child who has been waiting, often for a year or more, for someone they can look up to. This broke my heart.

Over the last decade, I have seen this time and again. People view volunteering as something that is "nice to do," not "need to do." When something more important or interesting comes along, they easily walk away from the volunteer commitment they made. They do not see the disappointment on a child's face who was counting on them to show up, or the lurch they put a nonprofit in that was counting on them for their time and service. Nonprofits are short-staffed as it is (which is why volunteers are critical to their ability to transform communities and lives) and they need to be able to count on people who do what they say they will do, when they say they will do it. To truly understand the value of a volunteer to a nonprofit, it's worth 4 minutes of your time to watch this video made for my client and friend, SoléAna Stables:

If your primary motivation to volunteer is that it would be additive to your resume, just don't. Don't beat yourself up about it, either. There are two kinds of people in the world: givers and takers. While we all have a little of both in us, we are predominantly one or the other, and the world needs both. But if you make a commitment, follow through—especially if you have made a commitment to a child.

Also, recognize that you are not a savior. Good volunteers meet those with whom they are working where they are without judgment or pretense. It's wonderful to open up the view of possibilities for someone who has a limited worldview (one of my favorite questions is, "What if I could show you how?"), but remember that your values and beliefs may vary dramatically from those with whom you are working, and it does not make their values or beliefs wrong. I remember when I moved to Spain in 1999. As the bus from Madrid to Ronda made its only stop at the halfway point, our director got on the loudspeaker and said, "When you use the restroom in Spain, do not flush the toilet paper—no matter what! It doesn't matter what's on the toilet paper, do not flush it. The sewer system is not designed for that. Place the paper in the trash can beside the toilet. This may sound gross, but throughout your time here, remember: It's not better or worse—it's just different." Since that day, every time I'm confronted with something that doesn't align with my values and beliefs, I remind myself it's not better or worse; it's just different.

I was matched with a Little relatively quickly. I had also signed up to become a pen-pal through The Order of Malta, a Catholic organization that matches writers with prison inmates. The letters run through The Order of Malta; we use first names only, and we do not share any identifying information with our pen-pals. We simply write one letter a month with a message of encouragement, a picture of a landscape, and a scripture, to an inmate with whom we are matched, regardless of whether they ever write back.

Just show up. That is all it takes to be a mentor to a child and give hope to someone with little to hope for each day. It was through all this volunteer work that I realized the second quality I possess that made me professionally successful. I show up.

I show up when it's easy, like calling a donor to thank them for a gift or surprising an employee with a bonus. I show up when it's hard, like calling my boss to tell her I lost a six-figure gift or promoting an employee who is no longer adding value to the organization to the market (also known as firing or a reduction in force). I show up when it's meaningful to the other person, like a baptism, and when it's fun, like a birthday party. Just show up. No one cares if you have the right words, wore the right thing, or if you brought the right gift. They care that you are there. That you are present. That you are communicating.

How many times have we heard the expression, "Do what you say you're going to do when you say you're going to do it"? How many people actually do that? I am still amazed by how many people cannot follow through on the promises and commitments they make.

> At the end of the day, what separates leaders from everyone else is not intelligence, letters after your name, or your network, but the ability to deliver on the promises you make.

How well do you do what you say you will do when you say you will do it? In other words, how reliable are you?

It is hard to believe that all it really takes to get ahead and for your team to succeed is to set reasonable goals for yourself and those around you and then meet those goals. Whether you lead a team of hundreds in a corporate setting, are a schoolteacher, a stay-at-home parent, a student, or maybe serve on a nonprofit board, you lead people every day. As a leader, I have always had the innate ability to help people break down goals into reasonable pieces and to inspire and empower them to achieve at their highest level. My ability to do that is aided when I am meeting with people face-to-face. Even though the world has changed and become more interconnected through video conferencing software like Zoom and Teams, there is still no substitution for face-to-face interaction.

After three years of working remotely and commuting with Mercy Home, I knew I was doing a disservice to my team. I was in the wrong seat on the bus, and it was time for me to take a seat farther back, making room for another leader to head to the front. After an open and honest discussion with my boss, I worked with my Associate Director of Philanthropy to transition all of my managerial and leadership responsibilities to him. My new role would be supporting him as he assumed greater human resource ownership and cultivating, soliciting, and stewarding gifts for the organization.

As my life in Houston grew, my day-to-day involvement at Mercy Home seemed to lessen by the hour, and I once again felt like maybe I was no longer on the right bus. When I tried to talk to my husband about my ever-growing sense of not belonging, he would remind me, "You earn a great salary, the benefits are amazing, you have all the flexibility you could want or hope for, you love your donors, you believe in the mission… What is the problem?"

It's difficult to explain. My husband was right. Most people are willing to tolerate their threads of discontent to stay in a role that is known and offers stability—financially and professionally. Every morning, you wake up, get ready for work, hop on the bus, and sit in your regular window seat, third row from the front. Life has become so repetitive that you are now on autopilot, unaware that deep down you feel defeated and lost. When was the last time you stopped to think, *Is this really the seat I want to be sitting in? Is this bus going to the destination I'm trying to get to? Heck, am I even on the right bus?*

It was 2018, and after four years in Houston, I had built a solid network of friends and acquaintances, especially in the philanthropic community. Several of my friends were working as nonprofit consultants and were encouraging me to become a consultant.

"There is a shortage of consultants with your business and planned giving background," they told me. "You're doing amazing work, but for one nonprofit. Think of the impact you could make as a consultant, working with multiple nonprofits."

When I thought about it, I felt alive again. I did not know how I would make it work financially (it's not like I had a pipeline of nonprofits eager to work with me), so I did what I had always done when faced with a bus transfer: I asked for help.

I called my mentor, Mimi, who had since left Mercy Home and assumed the role of President & CEO at Boys & Girls Clubs of Chicago. We set a date for dinner, I booked a flight to Chicago, and over a meal, I shared with her what I was thinking of doing. She was fully supportive of me leaving Mercy Home, and she was fully supportive of me going into consulting.

In fact, overwhelmingly, she said, "Angie, I think you would be so good. It would be a perfect fit for you." Since I knew nothing about consulting and had no prospective clients, my plan was to join someone else's consulting practice. That was the one piece of the plan Mimi said she did not support. "It would be a mistake for you to join someone else's practice. You should start your own business."

I felt small. Tentatively I said, "I don't know anything about starting a business."

She looked at me like I had three heads and said, "Well, you'll figure it out."

"I don't have any clients."

Confidently and with a tone as if to say, 'this conversation is over,' she said, "You'll figure that part out too."

Okay! I thought. *If Mimi thinks I can do it, then I will prove her right!* Just as I had borrowed Bill's confidence in me at Smith Barney, Jon's confidence in me at Principal, Greg's confidence in me in high school, and Mr. Brems' confidence in me in junior high, I borrowed Mimi's confidence in me until I could find my own.

I don't know that any of us ever outgrow our imposter syndrome. I cycle through feelings of inadequacy several times a year. Borrowing someone else's belief in us until we can stop sitting and spinning in our own heads is the fastest route back to the road of success and fulfillment. Over the years, I have wondered if I would be more successful if I got an MBA or my CFRE (Certified Fund Raising Executive). Higher education and initials after my name are not me. I have a wider range of experience, knowledge, and expertise from years of hard work, research, and self-education than most of my credentialed peers. If credentials are what's most important to a client, then I am not the consultant for them. If the ability to deliver and help an organization grow is important to a client, then I am the consultant for them.

I quit my job the next day. I had no business. I had no business name. I had no clients. I had no revenue. I gave 30 days' notice and returned home to Houston.

"How was your trip?" my husband asked.

"I quit my job," I replied.

"Why would you do that?" he asked.

"I wasn't happy anymore. I want to have a greater impact."

"You made more impact than most of us ever will. No job is going to be perfect," he said.

"I know that, but I think God is calling me to do something greater. I'm starting my own consulting firm."

"How many clients do you have?"

"None."

"How much money are you going to make?"

"I really don't know," I said truthfully.

Some have said I didn't take much of a risk quitting a secure job to start my own business because I am, in full disclosure, married to someone who is successful in his own right. There is comfort in that. Here's what you need to know about me: I am fiercely independent. I pay my own bills, my portion of taxes, and save for my own retirement. In fact, I'm so stubbornly independent that my husband and I do not even have a joint account.

Nothing in life is certain, and after my divorce, I made the decision that I would never be financially tied to another human ever again. So yeah. Quitting a stable job to start my own business was risky and scary to me. Call it ego or hubris, but my worst nightmare is having to go to my husband and say, "I failed. Can you bail me out?" This attitude forces me to be the best I can be for my clients. You won't make it long in consulting if your clients do not experience success—especially when the majority of your business is word of mouth. I am proud to say that every client I work with who follows the plan has doubled their revenue within 12-18 months of implementation.

My last week at Mercy Home for Boys & Girls, I reached out to my best donors (those who had become my friends) as well as some of the board members to whom I had grown close. One of those board members is a gentleman named Bob. Bob is the founder and owner of Diana's Bananas. You may have seen them in the frozen food section of your local supermarket. If you like chocolate-covered bananas, I highly recommend them. Available in milk and dark chocolate!

"Bob," I said, "it's been such a pleasure getting to know you and working with you over the years. I felt I owed it to you to tell you, personally, that I've tendered my resignation to Mercy Home."

"What are you going to be doing?" Bob asked.

"I'm starting my own business."

He kind of chuckled, "You know, I have one piece of advice for you."

"What's that?"

"Starting your business feels a little like building an airplane from scratch as you're flying it. When you finish, there will be a whole box of spare parts. Don't worry about the spare parts. Just keep the plane in the air and you'll be fine."

Lessons Learned:

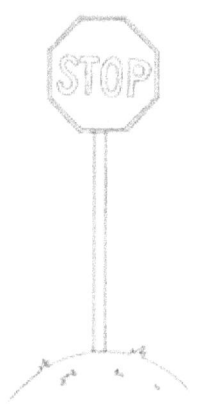

1. *It's not better or worse; it's just different.*
2. *What separates leaders from everyone else is not intelligence, letters after your name, or your network, but the ability to deliver on the promises you make.*
3. *Just keep the plane in the air.*

CHAPTER THIRTEEN

Driving the Bus

As a business owner, you are wholly responsible for the bus and all of its contents. You own the bus. You fuel the bus. You maintain the bus. You drive the bus. You sell bus tickets. You navigate, decide who gets on, make sure everyone stays safely in their seats at all times, and escort passengers off when warranted.

I made a quick decision on a business name. It is shockingly hard to come up with something that isn't already spoken for. "Just use your name or your initials," everyone told me. I did not like that idea for two reasons. First, I have seen how this plays out with successful businesses. When the owner (whose name or initials ARE the brand) wants to retire or sell, clients get nervous. Second, I wanted a business name that meant something.

I settled on Broad Oaks Consulting. In Houston, broad oak trees line so many picturesque neighborhoods, creating breathtaking canopies and shady retreats for the community. It's shocking that rapidly growing areas, paved in so much concrete, could also be the home of these impressive oaks, some dating back more than 300 years.

For generations, someone has seen enough value in these magnificent trees to grow them, protect them, steward them, and prop them up. Progress did not overtake them.

Broad Oaks Consulting was chosen because we see the value in nonprofits that serve our community and the people and institutions who support them. Step by step, we help our clients preserve and grow so that just like those trees that beautify our community, they may continue their work making the world a better place to live.

With our name in place, it was time to start getting a pipeline of clients going. I called my friend, Sara—one of the nonprofit consultants who had been encouraging me to make the leap to consulting in Houston—and said, "Sara, I did it. I took the plunge. I quit my job, and I'm starting my own company. I have no clients. I have no idea what I'm doing. But you've really been encouraging me in this direction, and I just wanted to say, 'thank you.'"

"That's fantastic!" She said, "And as a matter of fact, I have three or four prospective clients who have made inquiries with me. I don't have the capacity to work with them at the moment, and I'd love to introduce you."

With Sara's referral, I landed one of my very first clients, The Landing, an organization that walks alongside survivors of human trafficking and sexual exploitation. We live in a "do-it-yourself" society, but when we let others in, when we thank them for the ways in which they have inspired us, and when we ask for help, most of the time we find support. You never get what you don't ask for.

That first contract paid $1,500 a month for six months. The question quickly became, is it even worth it by the time I paid taxes?

"This is just a stepping stone," I promised my husband. I repeated one of Dr. Pfau's principles to myself over and over again:

Think and act as if it were impossible to fail.

I was worried I didn't really know what I was doing, but as I listened to The Landing's challenges and began to understand their needs, I naturally began applying my years of experience in growing for profit businesses to their framework: Assess needs and gaps from a cross-section of constituents (a standard S.W.O.T., or Strengths, Weaknesses, Opportunities, Threats, analysis), summarize the findings, make recommendations, get buy-in, develop a growth plan, and empower them to execute.

I love to be surrounded by things that fill me with inspiration, and one of the pieces of artwork in my office is a Spiritile with a bluebird and the words, *What if I fall? Oh, but what if you fly?* on it. You will never realize your potential unless you take the leap.

I made connections, got referrals, joined different networks, and more and more business began rolling in. While my intention in starting Broad Oaks was to center my services around planned giving, it quickly became apparent most nonprofits are not ready for a planned giving program. After all, you must learn to walk before you can learn to run.

Houston is home to more than 22,000 nonprofits. Approximately 92 percent of nonprofits operate on a budget of less than $1 million a year. Larger, more established consulting firms compete for the 8 percent of nonprofits who can afford to stroke big checks for outside counsel. I remembered a conversation I had with my mom earlier that year when I was applying to speak at a conference. It was the first time I was putting myself out there as an expert in philanthropy, and I was trying to come up with something that really built me up in the technical, advanced planning space.

"I understand that this is your area of expertise, but how many people will be at this conference that are actually ready for that information? How many of them know enough about the basics of fundraising to attend one advanced planning session, return home, and make big changes for their organization?"

She had a point. "What would you do?" I asked.

"I know it probably doesn't seem as exciting, but what if you offered a 'basics' session? It would certainly appeal to a broader audience."

She was right. As I thought about my need to generate business, I realized that I'd rather build something that fits 92 percent of nonprofits than 8 percent. If I was successful in helping small nonprofits build a solid foundation in fundraising on which they could grow, they would return as repeat clients when they were ready to elevate their fundraising once again. You see, nonprofits *are*, in fact, very much like small businesses. They just have a different tax status and motivation than their for profit counterparts.

When nonprofits have a strategic development plan their organization can actually execute, when marketing and fundraising (sales) work together in concert, and when they are successful in their mission (do what they say they are going to do), and show their donors their appreciation (stewardship), they will experience rapid growth like any small business.

Think about it. For any small business to succeed, it needs:

1. A value-added product.
2. A plan.
3. Marketing/Sales.
4. Operations.
5. Great customer service.

Once those pieces are in place, working in concert, the next logical step is scalability. Major and planned gifts are what allow successful nonprofits to scale. If, instead of going elephant hunting, I were willing to go duck hunting, my odds of growing my own practice rapidly increased dramatically, and I would help nonprofits become long-term sustainable, aligning with Broad Oaks' mission.

In my first two years, my clients were smaller, social service-oriented nonprofits. I found a niche here. It was eye-opening to see how these tiny organizations (The Landing's annual revenue was just $580,000 when we started work at the end of 2018) were changing our community and, quite literally, saving lives. Over the last several years, I have come to the realization that every major societal issue we have—poverty, income disparity, educational divides, hunger, abuse, human trafficking, affordable housing, animal rescue, drug addiction, and mental health—is addressed primarily by nonprofits. Every natural disaster, flood, fire, or tornado is met with teams of nonprofits and volunteers.

"Not true!" You may be thinking. "Our government takes care of those needs through my tax dollars."

You are only partially correct. Our government allocates money to address these, and other, issues, but do you know how the money actually reaches the intended recipient? Nonprofits. Nonprofits apply for funding from those allocations and administer the distribution. Nonprofits offer the services.

In late 2019, my consulting practice reached a turning point. I had a contact at the University of Houston, and one day she reached out to me and asked if I might be able to help out on a small contract for the University of Houston Bauer College of Business. It was small for them, but it felt like a major stepping stone for me.

When that contract came through, I was so excited. I called my friend, Brooke (the one who gave me the book *Hope for the Flowers* when we graduated high school), and said, "You're never going to believe this! This is huge! It is sure to be a resume builder for me!" In the end, this contract did not magically launch my practice to new heights, but I share this story with you because of what my friend Brooke did.

She sent me a bouquet of flowers, and in the bouquet was a lapel pin of a white horse. The card read, *"In a sea of unicorns, be a workhorse."* In a world where it seems everyone wants to be a special and unique unicorn, it's the workhorses that get things done! Little did she know my husband and I often describe our days in horse terms, despite the fact that we've never owned horses or spent time around horses.

"How was your day?" I'll ask.

"I was a Clydesdale," he'll reply. Clydesdales are workhorses, meaning he worked hard and got a lot accomplished. Some days we are racehorses, other days we are Clydesdales, still others we are Seabiscuit, lounging underneath a tree, sleeping throughout the entire day.

Her enclosure read, *"You've worked so hard to get to where you are. I'm so proud of you. Congratulations."* I cried. We don't spend enough time celebrating others' success. I think it's human nature to look at a big accomplishment someone else has made and feel inferior. I feel it all the time. I am part of a networking group made up of highly successful, high-achieving people around the world. Every day I look at their posts and think, "I'll never compete with that."

Of course, I won't! Primarily because it's not a competition. We're all on different roads, taking different buses. Every time I see something someone else has done that fills me with feelings of inadequacy or even jealousy, I immediately congratulate them on their success and celebrate them. When we celebrate one another, joy follows. Joy negates feelings of jealousy and allows you to be truly happy for others for what they've accomplished.

It was the end of 2019, and my business was thriving. I had built a six-figure business in less than a year, but with seven clients at year-end, I felt like the wheels were coming off. Despite tax law changes and the fact that most Americans no longer itemize, December is still the single largest month for giving (fun fact: more money is given to charity on December 31 than any other day of the year). Consequently, for nonprofits to get their message heard, they need aggressive campaigns to compete for dollars. Running year-end campaigns for seven nonprofits by myself at the same time was exhausting. I knew I could not have another year-end like that again, but I had no plan. Still, I had 10 months to figure it out.

Then the pandemic hit. As the world came to a screeching halt and uncertainty loomed, it appeared that everyone—individuals and nonprofits alike—were tightening their purse strings in preparation for the worst. I was

100 percent certain the first expense to go would be nonprofit consultants. *So much for my budding business*, I thought.

If business was to slow down, maybe this would be an opportunity for me to do something that had been on my bucket list. One of my donors at Mercy Home had told me about her volunteer work as a court-appointed Guardian ad Litem (GALs). GALs, or Casa Workers, act as the voice of a foster child in court. When you talk about groups of people getting the shaft, foster kids are at the top of the list. When Joanne shared with me what she was doing, I was in awe. She was helping kids navigate a broken system and giving them an actual shot at life. She also shared how much of her time it took. It was basically a part-time job.

As we all took to our homes and in anticipation of a slowdown in business, I decided to recommit to volunteer work and signed up for the 40-hour GAL training through Child Advocates in Houston. The training was clunky (Zoom was new) and the homework was intense. About a month later, I was sworn in by a judge and I took on my first case.

The bus began to accelerate quickly. I started to feel as though at every bus stop, I only had time for a rolling stop, rather than a complete stop. Instead of people getting on in an orderly fashion, it felt like cats were jumping on, and I was trying to herd dozens of them while keeping my eyes (and the bus) on the road.

One of my clients in early 2020 was RaiseUp Families, and in April of that year, their Executive Director (ED) was offered a phenomenal opportunity at Rice University. I had been working with them since July 2019 and was the only person who knew the organization as well as she did. When she submitted her resignation, the board asked if I would be willing to step in as Interim ED to ensure a smooth transition. Funding had decreased by almost half in the last year and with this latest hit, the board had decided perhaps it was time to merge RaiseUp Families with another, larger nonprofit in town.

I loved RaiseUp. I first learned about them in 2015, shortly after I had moved to Houston, and I fell in love with their organization because they treat the cause, not the symptom. They stabilize parents from vulnerable communities who face unexpected financial crises so their children can focus on their education, giving them the opportunity for a better life. Want kids to stay in school? Make sure parents stay in housing. Want less dependency on public services? Help adults get better paying jobs and teach them how to manage money. Plus, they had been tracking their outcomes since 1994, a rarity in the nonprofit space.

I said "yes" to the Interim ED role, but rather than merge the organization with another, the board and I grew it. By June of 2020, the pandemic in full-force, I was navigating this new and tenuous time as the ED of a RaiseUp Families, had one other nonprofit client, SoléAna Stables, who provided equine-assisted therapeutic riding to people with special needs, and I was working with one foster child who had been removed from her mother's care due to drug abuse and neglect.

It was a lot at the time. While I had managed teams of 200 at Morgan Stanley, raised over $15 million a year for Mercy Home as the head of its largest fundraising arm, and done some emotionally challenging volunteer work, I had never been solely responsible for a small business, its employees, and all the people that business served. People forget that eviction stays and government assistance did not happen immediately. If I did not raise $650,000, the five employees working for me would lose their jobs, families would lose their homes, and children would have huge gaps in their education, setting them on an even more challenging path for the future. Not only that, if I did not help my other client, SoléAna Stables, weather the storm, their organization would go under, and 7 years of work would be reduced to a pile of rubble. Activity restrictions and the fragile health of those they served prevented them from offering Riding lessons—their core program.

It was a lot of pressure, and I found the strength to keep going through my relationship with God, my network of support, and my volunteer work with Child Advocates. The foster child I was assigned to was 6, and I had to build a relationship with her over FaceTime and the phone because we were not permitted to see the children entrusted to our care in person. When she was removed from her mother, she was placed with her maternal aunt, a lovely human. Talk about people who are inspiring! The aunt was single, in her mid to late 20s, and worked as a special-needs school teacher. She took her niece on with the ferocity of a mama bear, committed to providing every resource and therapy possible to give her niece a happy and healthy life. If she could take on a troubled child as a schoolteacher in the midst of a pandemic and keep a positive attitude, I could raise $650,000, keep people employed, prevent families from becoming homeless, and save a nonprofit. Once again I found myself borrowing confidence from other people when my own confidence was waning. If I wouldn't have opened my heart and made room in my life for this volunteer work, I never would have met this amazing woman who still inspires me every day to know that I can do more and be a better human.

The case closed about a year later when the angel aunt adopted the young girl, and I took on my second case. This case was complicated. There were three siblings ages 11, 14, and 16 living in 2 different homes, and the 11-year-old and 16-year-old were both intellectually and developmentally disabled (I/DD). As a GAL, you are required to have a 360-degree view of the child and everyone in their life, which means that every month you need to connect with:

1. The child
2. The foster parent
3. The biological parent (if family reunification is the goal)

4. Their teachers
5. Their therapists
6. Their caseworker (Child Protective Services)

I was also required to attend parent-teacher conferences as well as ARD, or Admission, Review, and Dismissal, meetings for both of my I/DD children and work with their teachers to develop an IEP, or Individualized Education Program, for each child. I do not have children. The last time I was in a classroom was when I was in school. I had absolutely no idea how to help these kids, and as difficult as it is to navigate the foster care system, it's 10 times harder to navigate for a child with I/DD.

I remember the feeling of overwhelm taking over one day and calling my mom to say I did not know how I was going to do this. How was I going to learn everything I needed to know to help these kids while running RaiseUp Families and maintaining a high quality of work and integrity with my other clients?

"Maybe this is the time you acknowledge that you can't do everything. I know your heart is in the right place, but maybe this is just something you can't do. Maybe even you have a limit."

Logically, I know we all have limits. But to the core of my being, I embrace Dr. Pfau's Principle #1: *Whatever the mind can conceive and the heart can believe can be achieved.* A few weeks later, I got together with a friend I hadn't seen in a long time. She had gone through a complicated and heartbreaking divorce years earlier and was back in court with her ex-husband, trying to get full custody of her boys. I told her about the pressure I was under and that I thought maybe I needed to step away from my volunteer work so I could focus on my paid work. It seemed like the practical thing to do.

"Angela, you're doing A LOT. I get that it's overwhelming. Your work with RaiseUp Families and SoléAna Stables is changing so many lives. But of all the things you do, the largest single impact you will make in this world is for those kids. There are a lot of nonprofit consultants out there. Give up business before you give up on those kids."

I knew she was right. When I commit to something, I am all in. And I needed to be all in for these kids. Removed from their biological mom when they were all under 10, and placed with a foster mom who later adopted them, she proceeded to move them outdoors. They became outdoor children, living in a gazebo in the backyard, after the adoption went through. They were only allowed indoors in the evening for dinner, to shower, and to sleep. When school went virtual during the pandemic, teachers made the discovery.

The system and everyone in it had let these kids down time and again. I knew I would never be able to live with myself if I passed them off, like everyone else had because it was too much work. As my rapport with the older two grew, they would regularly send me text messages saying, "Ms. Angela, you're the nicest person we've ever met." *Houston: We have a problem.* If I'm the nicest person someone has met by the time they're a young adult, we have issues.

Once again, Dr. Pfau's principles were ringing in my ears. As part of his training, he made every participant memorize and repeat a quote from Vince Lombardi:

"The quality of a person's life is in direct proportion to their commitment to excellence, regardless of their chosen field of endeavor."

It's not surprising that people get confused about what I do for a living. Many people think that because my husband is successful in his own right and I work with nonprofits, I volunteer all day. "It's nice that you have something to keep you busy while Gary's at work," they say. Some people think I'm a social worker. Most people think I'm primarily the Executive Director of RaiseUp Families, and I have a little "side hustle" with Broad Oaks Consulting.

I still struggle with what to say when someone asks me what I do for work, and if I had to sum it up in one word, it would probably be "Philanthropist." Merriam-Webster defines "philanthropist" as "one who makes an active effort to promote human welfare." Perhaps my favorite definition of "philanthropist" is "a person who donates time, money, experience, skills, or talent to help create a better world," on fidelity.com. Both agree the Greek root of philanthropy may be literally translated as "loving people."

I do not have one chosen field of endeavor. I am a business owner, a nonprofit leader, a coach, a volunteer, a mentor, a wife, a published author, a speaker, a daughter, a Godmother, a sister, an athlete, and a friend—all at the same time. The quality of my life is in direct proportion to my commitment to fulfilling each of those roles with excellence because I CAN (Constant And Neverending Improvement).

Determined to raise the bar at RaiseUp Families, I began reevaluating the program and quickly realized I needed help. It was 2021, and since 1994, RaiseUp Families had a track record of helping families increase their household income by an average of 35-40 percent while in their core, 9-month HandUp program (if you want to learn more about RaiseUp, visit raiseupfamilies.org). I had raised $954,000 in private donations in my first year with the organization, but our family outcomes were no better than they had been in the previous five years. As I looked at what a 35-40 percent income increase meant in mean household income, I realized families were making an average of about $26,000, after the increase. We can do better. We need to do better. If you're trying to raise a family on $26,000, it doesn't matter how good your savings habits are. You will never get ahead.

I'm a voracious reader (okay, confession: I'm an audiobook junkie), and that summer, two books would end up changing the course of life for parents in RaiseUp's HandUp program. The first was the historical fiction book, *The Four Winds* by Kristin Hannah, and the second was *The Unspoken Rules: Secrets to Starting Your Career Off Right* by Gorick Ng.

I had been mulling over why RaiseUp's clients were working some of the lowest-paying jobs in Houston, and as I read Ms. Hannah's novel, I realized it was because no one had ever shown them how to be successful in a different work environment where they could earn more, have upward mobility, and access benefits.

As I pondered how to provide them with those skills, someone who followed RaiseUp on Facebook introduced me to the Executive Director of Atlas Scholars, thinking there would be a natural partnership between our agencies. At our second meeting, Jenna Moon gave me a copy of Gorick's book, *The Unspoken Rules*.

Jenna and I had a long talk that day about poverty and income, and that's when I first learned about the happiness index as it relates to income. The premise is that once people are making between $60,000-$75,000 a year (depending on where they live), they reach a maximum happiness level and do not become incrementally happier once that income level is exceeded. The reason is that with an income between $60-75k, most people have enough to pay their bills, save, and have enough left over for some discretionary spending. All that changes as income increases is discretionary spending gets greater, and as we all know, money cannot buy happiness.

If I could teach people how to navigate the workplace, they would have the ability to reach the happiness index. Gorick had shown me how and my new vision for RaiseUp Families was to have 50 percent of their graduating families reach a median household income of $60,000 or more within three years of entering RaiseUp's 9-month signature HandUp program. Armed with Gorick's book about demonstrating competency, commitment, and compatibility in the workplace, all I needed to do was start a book club. I could teach the nuts and bolts, but I needed someone who could help clients develop mental fortitude, self-regulation skills, and build their confidence.

I began interviewing people, but no one was a fit. Then one day in mid-September, the two Case Managers I had at RaiseUp Families both resigned on the same day, giving only 2 weeks' notice after 10 years of service. They had pulled the cord and were ready to exit the bus at the next stop.

People come; people go. It's the nature of work and of being the boss. I needed to restaff, but I had no idea what kind of people I was looking for or how I would train them. I needed help. Fast. I needed Telisa Mason (ne: Dixon).

Telisa and I had worked together at Mercy Home in Chicago, she in direct care with youth, and I in development. Because it was a residential facility, we had a big, shared cafeteria staff dined in for lunch every day (by the way, free lunch every day was a HUGE benefit of working at Mercy Home). Most people stuck to their own groups or teams when it came to who they sat with at lunch. It was a lot like elementary, middle, and high school.

I'm sure it will come as no surprise that I frequently went over to a table full of people I did not know and said, "Hi! I'm Angela. I work in Development. May I join you for lunch?" Sometimes I received a "No, we're having a team meeting," but most of the time, people were happy to have me join.

Telisa and I became fast friends, and what I knew about her was that she was (and is) an amazing therapist and social worker. Her ability to understand people, to put them at ease, to normalize their fears, anxieties, and emotions, and then help them develop tiny micro habits they can start with to break out of whatever cycle is holding them back is uncanny. I needed Telisa to be my partner if I was going to rebuild the Case Management team and affect the kind of life-altering change I envisioned for RaiseUp Families.

She had since relocated from Chicago to Dallas and, to my delight, when I called and asked her if she would be willing to move to Houston to come work with me, she said yes!

There was so much work to be done at RaiseUp, for SoléAna Stables, and for a new client I had signed in March. Not only that, but my GAL volunteer work was also taking somewhere between 20-30 hours a month, depending on the month, and year-end was approaching once again.

This isn't a sustainable business model, I kept repeating. *Something has to change.* I had tried outsourcing some of the writing and creative work I do for clients earlier in the year, but it was hard to find someone who could meet my expectations and, consequently, those of my clients. Gifted writers and asset creators (photo, video, image) are hard to come by. I was dreading year-end. It's my busiest time of year, and it's also football season. My husband and I go to every Texas Longhorns home game in Austin, and it's also gala season in the nonprofit world. In short, it's exhausting, and I was exhausted just thinking about it.

Every day, some new challenge arose. I was still getting my arms around running a nonprofit, creating policies and procedures, interviewing new staff members, and trying to develop my board of directors. The fiscal year had started over, and I needed to raise another $950,000 to keep the place running. Plus, the housing and rental crisis was far from over. It felt like the bus was going 70 miles an hour through the mountains, around a curve, and I was just holding on for dear life, praying we all made it safely to the end of the year without crashing.

Then one day in late October, the seeds of change were planted once again, this time through a podcast. The audiobook I was listening to had ended, and I didn't have another one teed up. I listen while I complete mundane tasks like my hair and makeup, laundry, or housework. I got out of the shower and just wanted something quick and light to make doing my hair and makeup more tolerable. For the first time in my life, I opened up the Apple Podcast app, randomly picked a category and podcast, and hit "play."

I have no idea what the podcast was or who the podcaster was, but whoever she was, she interviewed a woman I had also never heard of named Dorie Clark. The podcast changed the way I saw my future. I knew I needed Dorie on my bus. One of the projects I started at RaiseUp was tightening up our volunteer application. I reached out to a well-known area nonprofit that serves a similar population to RaiseUp but in a different way. They have an exceptionally robust volunteer program, and I asked if they would share their application with me. "No," they responded. "It's proprietary." Give me a break! It's a list of questions.

One of the first things Dorie said in this podcast interview was something to the effect of, "Nothing drives me crazier than people's unwillingness to share. I don't think you can put enough free content out there when we're all just trying to get better." I remember standing in my bathroom and thinking, *Yes, I think this woman and I are kindred spirits.*

The other quality that immediately drew me to Dorie was that she was like me. She doesn't have a million initials behind her name. She didn't go to business school or law school, then work for prestigious firms like Goldman Sachs or McKenzie Group—all accomplishments I felt were holding me back from being recognized as an expert in my field. She has a varied background including a theology degree from Harvard, a few years working at a nonprofit, and yet she has become an internationally recognized business thought leader with over 300,000 followers on LinkedIn; she changed careers, took risks, and gained her skills through hard work, determination, and experience. She did more in helping me overcome my own imposter syndrome in 40 minutes than I had managed to do for myself in the last five years. At the conclusion of the interview, I immediately downloaded her book, *The Long Game*. The next morning, I went for a walk and began listening when something clicked in my brain again.

I can rework my business and do something that's never been done before. If I do this, I will add greater value to my clients, help them raise more money, gain more awareness, and reduce the number of hours I spend with each client by 80 percent, I thought. As my contracts with clients last anywhere from 6-18 months and I was a one-person shop, I had only worked with 10 clients up to this point. Six of the ten had experienced 100 percent or greater revenue growth within 12-18 months of signing with me. What was it that made those 6 successful and the other 4 fail miserably? We are our own worst critics, and for a long time, I had believed that it was something I had failed to do that prevented my 4 clients from succeeding.

I went back and reviewed every client diligently. My process was the same every time. While all client's growth opportunities are different, the underlying methodology, or framework, is always the same. As I looked deeper, the reason the laggards did not make it was simple:

1. Failure to execute on the plan (in other words, they did not do what I told them to do).
2. Lack of clarity in messaging and marketing.

I knew what I needed to do, but I needed time to do it. In November 2021, I went to all of my clients except for two and exercised the 30-day out clause in my contract so that I could begin rebuilding my business. I walked away from $70,000, which was not easy at the time, but I wanted to build something that would allow me to scale so that I could help even more nonprofits lay a foundation for growth. I remembered Matthew McConaughey sharing in his book *Greenlights* that he turned down romantic comedy roles for nearly 2 years—and *millions of dollars*, not tens of thousands—to be seen as something other than the "Rom-com" and "shirtless on the beach guy." Sure, Matthew McConaughey and I aren't exactly in the same league, but they're just commas and zeroes after all.

Lessons Learned:

1. *You never get what you don't ask for.*

2. *Your past experience is never lost or wasted; it's just repurposed.*

3. *You don't have to know someone to borrow their innovation or confidence; take it and make it your own.*

CHAPTER FOURTEEN

When the Bus Crashes

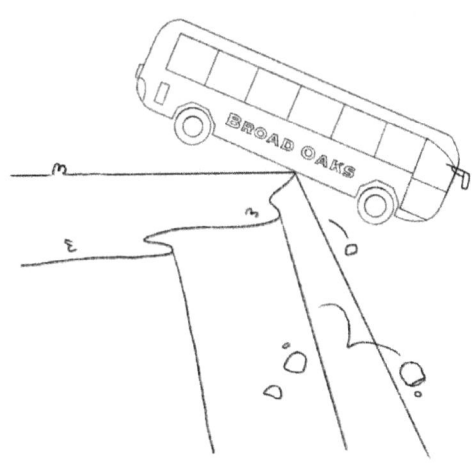

As 2021 drew to a close, I took nearly three weeks' vacation. I needed the break to reset and get prepared for what was sure to be an amazing year ahead. I had an idea for a great new business product. There was nothing like it on the market. It was going to be absolutely revolutionary for small nonprofits.

My model and inspiration for my new product, "Laying a Foundation for Growth" or "LFG" (https://layingafoundation.com), was Dorie Clark's "Recognized Expert" course. I had signed up for the course in November of the prior year and was learning as much by observing what she did as I was with the course itself. If it worked for her, there was no reason it couldn't work for me.

Telisa had hired 2 new Case Managers at RaiseUp Families to replace the old ones, and we were confident their skills and abilities would lead the organization to our desired client outcomes.

I returned from vacation completely refreshed and excited about the new year. As my head hit the pillow that night, I felt happy, relaxed, and at peace. The bus was full of gas. The course was charted. We had the right people in the right seats to reach our desired destination. The luggage was stored. We were ready. Nothing short of a tornado could stop us.

And that's exactly what happened. Sunday morning, I got a call from Telisa.

"I can't get into the office."

"What do you mean you can't get into the office?"

"I can't get in."

Dumbfounded, I said, "Just use the front door."

"No, you don't understand," she responded. "I can't get into the office. It's blocked off."

"Blocked off by who?"

"The police."

"Why?" I asked, confused.

And then she said it. The words that would cause the bus to not only crash but dangle off the side of a cliff for the better part of 2022. "The building got struck by a tornado last night."

A nasty storm had blown through the night before. On a positive note, no one was injured. On a negative note, this tornado literally touched down on one building in all of Houston—the building in which RaiseUp Families leased office space. Because the overall impact was so small, we got absolutely no news coverage, which made informing donors and every client families we were serving alike, a challenge. We did not have a backup plan; "in case of natural disaster" had never made its way into any policies and procedures.

I had 10 days to pack up 20 years' worth of stuff, much of which was now wet, and move it to storage. I knew we were going to outgrow that space in a year or two anyway, but zero planning had been done in considering where we might relocate. I knew nothing about commercial real estate and as I began the search for new space, I quickly learned I was facing an uphill battle. RaiseUp's work with the community requires physical space, so going all virtual was not an option.

With this mess to deal with, there was no way I could build LFG. I had already signed a new client to the platform, so I called to explain what had happened and asked if we could push our start date back to March. By the grace of God, she was very understanding and agreed.

By the end of January, I had found an amazing space that was in the same school district the old office had been (an important factor to some board members) and right off a major highway. When I met the building owner, he was nothing but gracious. "Angela, anything we can do to get you into this space, just let me know. We'll paint, we'll move walls, we'll put up walls, we'll put in a kitchen for you. Anything you want, we'll make it happen."

I left the site visit feeling good. The price was right, I was ready to begin contract negotiations, and the whole process had taken less than three weeks. Maybe this storm would turn out to be a blessing in disguise. We could get the extra space we desperately needed to grow the program.

When my phone rang and I saw it was my real estate broker, I eagerly picked up. "What's the good word?"

"We lost the lease."

"What? How?"

When the building owner found out RaiseUp works with families from vulnerable communities to stabilize them in their homes so their children can experience an education uninterrupted by eviction, he said, emphatically, "I don't want low-income people in my building," and pulled the option.

I was so disappointed. I looked at over 20 spaces in a matter of days, all of which were too far out, would take months to build out, or were too expensive. It was early February, and my team was beginning to unravel. Forcing them back to remote work was taking a toll on their mental health and their ability to serve clients. It was also impeding the goal to double the number of families served. We needed a plan and a space as soon as possible.

That first week of February 2022, COVID finally caught up with my husband and me. As we quarantined at home, I received a call from the real estate broker for the second lease RaiseUp was attempting to secure.

"We have a problem. The building found out that you work with low-income people, and they don't want low-income people in their building."

I thought, *You have to be kidding me. This is the second time this has happened. I don't understand it. Our clients are like anyone else.* 61% of Americans live paycheck-to-paycheck and pre-pandemic, the average American was $600 away from an eviction. As the pandemic wore on, many families coming to us for help had up to three months' expenses in savings prior to March 2020. When work becomes unreliable, when people stop earning steady income, when they don't have health insurance and they get sick, three months of expenses (let alone $600) doesn't last long.

I begged, I pleaded, and in the end, the building agreed to lease us the space. The build-out would begin soon, and the space would be move-in ready in early April. I built the "Laying a Foundation for Growth" framework and completed the first few modules. All I needed to do was stay one step ahead of my new client at any given time, and we would be in good shape.

As March rolled around, my volunteer work on the International Committee of the Houston Livestock Show and Rodeo began. The Houston Livestock Show and Rodeo is the single largest revenue-generating event in the state, is run by 35,000 volunteers, and proceeds from the Show provide scholarships for Texas kids to attend Texas colleges. During my first shift, I noticed my tongue felt strange. That's a weird thing to say, I know, that your tongue feels strange, but my tongue just hurt all day. When I woke up the next morning, it felt (and looked) like someone had put it through a meat grinder, and by the time I got out of the shower, I had lost all feeling and muscle control of the right side of my face. Concern that I was either having a stroke or a severe allergic reaction took me to a nearby emergency room clinic where I was misdiagnosed. By the next day, I was in tears. I couldn't eat or drink, I was in such excruciating pain.

A correct diagnosis came a few days later and I began the path to recovery, but no one was attending to the wrecked bus. I was out for 10 days as my weakened immune system left me with a nasty cold to boot. The first quarter of 2022 was over, and it was as though the bus had left the station and crashed in the first mile of our 1,000-mile journey.

Staff issues erupted at RaiseUp Families, causing me to question whether I had made the right hires. It was like I had been thrown through the windshield when the bus wrecked, but the passengers were still on the bus, a fight had broken out, and I could not do anything to break it up or get everyone back to their seats. For the first time in my life, I was doubting myself, my leadership quality, and questioning my choices. For the first time, I felt unsure of myself. I started to get concerned about what the board would think of me as a leader.

When we are faced with our own inadequacies—real or imagined—the easy thing to do is to push forward and hope for the best. The hard thing to do is to put our vulnerabilities out there. The hard thing is usually the right. I thought about the leaders I admired who had helped to form me. What would they tell me now? They would tell me to ask for help. Being vulnerable in the right moments is a sign of strength. No one wants a leader who believes themselves to be infallible.

As hard as it was, I went to the President and Vice President of the board and said, "I know I advocated so strongly to hire this person, but I'm not sure I made a good choice, and I'm worried about your confidence in me as a leader."

Their response changed my mindset about myself. They said, "You took a risk. It might not work out how you intended, but it can't erase years of good work and accountability."

It reminded me of what Bryan Stevenson said in his book *Just Mercy, A Story of Justice and Redemption*. "Each of us is more than the worst thing we've ever done." One bad decision or one risk you take that does not work out how you intended cannot erase your accomplishments and achievements.

What I learned in all of this is that our ability to succeed is more about owning our wrong turns and creating a plan to get the bus and its passengers back on course, than never having an accident to begin with. Accidents will happen; your bus will crash. It is your ability to regroup and start again that matters. What people crave most is direction and open communication.

As a leader, you do not need to have all the answers; you simply need to have a clear vision of where you are headed, the courage to be open and honest about the obstacles in the road, and the willingness to let others help you when you get stuck.

I have always been a person of faith, but as 2022 droned on, my relationship with God grew more and more important, my board members turned into some of my best friends, and my best friends gave me the extra push I needed to just make it through to the next day. I had felt called to all the choices I made after parting ways with Morgan Stanley. I could always hear God's calling in my life and responded, even when my initial thought was, *You want me to do what?* For the first time, I was questioning if I had misheard the message. If God wanted me to grow RaiseUp Families, why would my entire case management staff resign on the same day, my building get struck by a tornado, and my employees begin fighting uncontrollably? Why would I have had so many issues trying to find an office building that would offer a lease? Why would the United States Postal Service not deliver mail—mail that contains checks to continue our work—to the new offices? Maybe I had misheard the message. Maybe I was trying to force something into being that was not meant to be. Maybe I was not the leader I thought I was. Maybe I was on the wrong bus.

The demands on my time and attention kept growing. In addition to the challenges I was facing at RaiseUp, I had other clients who needed my expertise and energy. I had invested both capital and countless hours in Broad Oaks Consulting to create LFG, and while I still believed it would be revolutionary in our field, at the time, it was a drain. It was taking a toll on my health and my sanity.

By June 2022, RaiseUp Families' building crisis was over, and we were settled in new offices; staff tensions seemed to be easing; their annual fundraiser, "Graduation Celebration," was over and had outperformed every previous event by more than 100 percent; I had finished LFG, and it was ready to be marketed. I was over the moon. It felt like my first real "win" of 2022, and did I ever need a win! I was on this huge high, and I thought, *This is going to be so amazing!* Then, forty-eight hours later, rather than feeling accomplished, all I felt was defeat. It was a great product, but I had no new clients lined up to use it. I woke up at midnight on a Friday and went up to my office to look at the landing page again. It was beautiful, but with everything I had going on, where was I going to find time to market the program? If I didn't market it and sign new clients, then all the work I did would be for nothing. All I felt was failure. I was doubting my own ability to succeed. I crawled back into bed, next to my husband and started sobbing uncontrollably. He woke up, genuine concern in his voice.

"What's wrong?" he asked.

"I'm a failure!" I blurted out.

"What?"

"I'm never going to succeed."

"Stop being ridiculous," he said, groggily. "Just a few hours ago you were so excited about finishing your new project. Go back to sleep."

I suspect as you read this, you may be thinking the same thing my husband was: sounds like a highly emotional, gross overreaction. By all accounts, I should have been feeling accomplished, proud of the obstacles I had overcome, and the work I had done. It didn't feel that way. Since then,

I've learned about post-event adrenaline depression. Trial lawyers experience this very deeply and frequently. When you pour yourself into big projects for a prolonged period of time, you maintain a consistent adrenaline rush throughout the project. Your brain is being dosed in epinephrine all day, every day as you work through the crisis or project. The minute the project ends, the adrenaline that was keeping you going and focused stops; your body stops dosing your brain with large amounts of epinephrine and instead begins processing the chemical out. That process can cause a temporary depression. I thought there was something wrong with me. I now know there is nothing "wrong" with me. When I'm working on a big project (say, writing a book), I simply need to schedule a few days off one or two days post-completion to give my mind and body time to process and reset.

It felt like I had lived three years in the first half of 2022 and I had no idea how I was going to survive the next six months. Time seemed to move in slow motion. In July, I sat down with a colleague, Stephanie Hruzek, the Executive Director at Family Point Resources in Houston, and I told her everything. After I had finished, she looked me square in the eyes and said, "You know, most people would have given up. I'm surprised you kept going."

I wanted to give up so many times. I was exhausted, physically and mentally, at the end of each day. I fell asleep as soon as my head hit the pillow, but three hours later, I'd be wide awake, thinking about the staff at RaiseUp, the families we serve, and their children. *How was I going to raise $1.3 million dollars to meet the board's goal of doubling the number of families served in just one year?* I thought about my other clients. *Was I doing enough? Had I dropped the ball somewhere? Were there connections and opportunities I had inadvertently overlooked?* I thought about my foster kids. *How could I connect with the right people to afford them greater opportunities and a better life than what they had in their current placements? How could I find "forever homes" for them so that they were never returned to the system again? What would happen to them if I failed to find better solutions? Would I be able to live with* *myself?* I thought about my husband, his children, my parents, my grandmother, my brother, and my friends. *Had I missed birthdays, anniversaries, or milestones? When would I be able to get up to Iowa to see my parents and my 95-year-old grandmother? Was I showing up for everyone in my life in the right way at the right time? Was I delivering on the promises I had made to everyone in my life?* The opposite of showing up is letting down, and my fear of letting others down was getting the best of me. I felt a lot like Sarah Jessica Parker in the 2011 comedy, *I Don't Know How She Does It*, doing a million things, and few of them well.

How do you keep going when you have taken on more than you can handle? Throughout the second half of 2022, I reminded myself of something Tim Dwight, Sr., a teacher and our Vice Principal my senior year of high school, told me once: Anyone can do anything for a year. I could survive 2022, but something still had to give.

Lessons Learned:

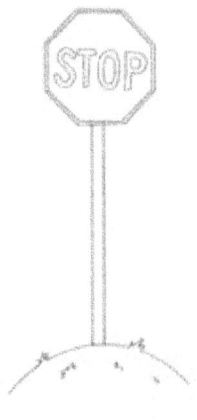

1. Being vulnerable in the right moments is a sign of strength. No one wants a leader who believes themselves to be infallible.

2. One bad decision or one risk you take that does not work out how you intended cannot erase your accomplishments and achievements.

3. Anyone can do anything for a year.

CHAPTER FIFTEEN

Scaling the Bus Line

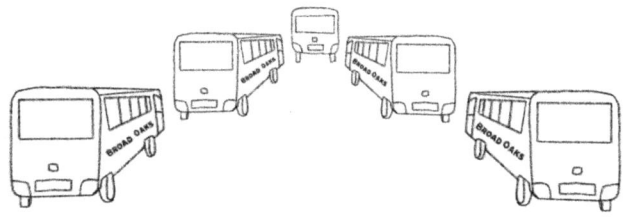

The idea for "Laying a Foundation for Growth" came when I read Dorie Clark's "The Long Game." In it, Dorie talks about a man named Dave who made the decision that he wanted to work no more than 30 hours a week and take two months off a year—July and December. I suspect many people who read this think, "Good luck, Dave! That's impossible if you want to be successful and make any money!"

When I read it, I thought, *that seems reasonable. If Dave can do it, so can I.* I have yet to achieve Dave's level of personal or financial freedom, but building LFG was the first step in the right direction. It was born out of a desire to remove the main obstacles nonprofits face in scaling their own growth (growing reliable revenue year after year), a desire to scale Broad Oaks Consulting, and the chance to offer myself more time and freedom to pursue content creation and speaking opportunities for the chance to have a greater, personal impact.

My vision was small when I started my company. I wanted to work with a handful of nonprofits each year on targeted projects and make roughly what I had been making when I was captive to Mercy Home. Basically, I wanted to change buses but stay in the same seat. After four years, my vision of my destination changed. I think there was a part of me that felt like dreaming beyond what I had already achieved was selfish and arrogant. Even now, in writing this autobiography, there's a voice inside me that says, "Who do you think you are? What, do you think you're special or something?"

On the recommendation of an acquaintance I met on a golf course in Hawaii, I picked up the book *The Mountain is You* by Brianna Wiest. Early on in the book, she talks about self-sabotage. "When we self-sabotage," she writes, "it is often because we have a negative association between achieving the goal we aspire to and being the kind of person who has or does that thing."

When I thought about my goal for Broad Oaks Consulting—to only serve a small contingency of nonprofits on targeted projects and to only earn at or slightly above what I was earning before—I realized I was self-sabotaging because of how I viewed people who experience wild financial success.

LFG was the first step in scaling the business, but it could be so much more. After five years of working with small nonprofits who are making a huge impact, my big dream is to help nonprofits of every size that are transforming our communities and our world to function like successful businesses and to shift the perception most people have of the nonprofit sector, empowering them to action. When I picture the kind of person who succeeds in this endeavor, I see her giving TedTalks, speaking at events, giving interviews, writing books, and charging a competitive fee for her knowledge and abilities. When I think of high income earners who spend their lives *talking* about doing good, rather than *doing* the actual "boots on the ground" work, I think of people who are fake, incompetent, and focused on enriching themselves. Why? Where did that perception come from? That certainly does not describe me.

Wiest explains, "Your self-concept is an idea that you have spent your whole life building. It was created by piecing together inputs and influences from those around you: what your parents believed, what your peers thought, what became self-evident through personal experience, and so on. Your self-image is difficult to adjust because your brain's confirmation bias works to affirm your pre-existing beliefs about yourself."

There's an expression, "those who can't do, teach," and it's one you hear a lot in wealth management. There is a commonly held belief that people get into leadership roles in that industry because they could not make it as agents or brokers. I never wanted to be thought of as someone who ended up leading because I was unable to do the work. As I examined my self-concept, I realized that as successful as I had been, I had put limitations on myself because, deep down, I felt like I needed to keep proving that I *can* do the work.

Give a man a fish, he'll eat for a day; teach a man to fish, he'll eat for a lifetime. I truly thought my process was a teaching process, but as I stepped back and evaluated it, I realized I had been doing all the work. I personally cleaned up my clients' data, did all their copywriting, and executed the development plans I wrote for them. I was essentially a development officer in every client's shop—proving I could do, rather than teach. Not only is that not scalable, it's not helpful. How could I help them learn the art and the science of growing a business in a way they could retain? How could I impart my years of knowledge and wisdom about fundraising and development to more clients, more efficiently? How could I duplicate myself?

The answer came by modeling Dorie Clark's "Recognized Expert" Course. The course is self-paced and once purchased, participants have lifetime access to it and all its contents. Once a month, there are REx meetings where RExers from around the globe get together to connect with other like-minded achievers, tackle challenges we are facing in our own endeavors, as well as celebrate our wins among a supportive group of peers.

LFG follows a similar model. It is a curriculum-based approach to consulting where clients learn the eight foundational pieces they need to know to scale their nonprofit. At the start of each contract, clients are assigned Module One. Once complete, we have a one-on-one coaching session to review the module and the associated homework. Then they have a week to implement. **Learning, coaching, implementation. Learning, coaching, implementation.**

Through this methodology, I can offer more information than I ever could in traditional meetings. Clients are less distracted and able to focus. Tedious tasks like data cleaning, audience segmentation, and building a story framework are broken into manageable pieces with guides and templates, rather than general information and strong suggestions. Because the content is recorded, they can go back into each learning module as often as they like to ensure they fully understand what we are doing and why.

Automating this critical learning freed up much of my time which made me wonder, *what is it that I'm not doing that I should be doing to help clients achieve even greater fundraising success?* One of the hardest things we as humans will ever do is look at what we're not good at and acknowledge our shortcomings. As you know by now, I'm keenly aware of my deficits and flaws.

I am not a visual person. I can tell a story that compels people to give, but I don't know how to captivate their attention in less than 6 seconds on a webpage. I don't even know how to build a web page. This is important because, statistically speaking, people are 60 percent more likely to visit a webpage and donate if they receive something in the mail. If a nonprofit sends a letter or a Development Officer tells a story at an event that compels a donor or prospective donor to visit the nonprofit website, if the site doesn't reinforce the message, captivate the user, call them to action, and make it easy for them to give, the probability of receiving a gift diminishes greatly.

Recognizing that most nonprofit websites are confusing, unclear, and clunky, as well as my own ineptitude in this area, I reached out to a former partner, Solace Media, to see if they would be willing to work with me and build a brand-new website for every "Laying a Foundation for Growth" client. As I'm working on fundraising and development, Solace Media helps our clients clarify their story, ensures their branding reinforces their messaging, and helps with email drip campaigns that work to cultivate, solicit, and steward donors.

For the same fee I had been charging for just fundraising and development work, Solace Media and Broad Oaks Consulting now offer a far superior product that gives nonprofits the ability to both fundraise and market effectively. Fundraising and marketing are like the two engines on an airplane. Sure, you can run on one for a while, but to make the long trip you need both to arrive safely.

Many of my competitors have looked at our product and said, "You could be charging double what you are for this. It's amazing." They are probably right, but both Solace Media and Broad Oaks Consulting see how tiny nonprofits have some of the biggest impacts in affecting change. We want our product to be accessible for them so that, like the oak trees that shade and beautify so much of Houston, they will still be around 100 years from now to serve or until every societal issue is eradicated.

With LFG up and running, I turned my attention to other downlines in my business. LFG is a six-month program that gets a nonprofit house in order so that they can begin to fundraise with efficiency and efficacy. It does not have a one-for-one return. In other words, simply completing LFG will not raise additional funds. It is in the execution of the Development Plan where meaningful growth happens, and that can take anywhere from 12-18 months. Not every client has the capacity to execute the development plan or the funding to hire a full-time Development Officer to do so. Further, given turnover issues in our industry, hiring carries its own risk until an organization is on stable ground.

This gave me the idea to launch a program called "Foundational Growth," where we execute client development plans for their first year or two after completing LFG, and to employ some exceptional writers and content creators to add a fresh perspective and scalability. This also comes with bi-weekly coaching sessions so that Executive Directors and Development Officers can be coached on building relationships with individual givers, cultivating, soliciting, and stewarding donors, successful event execution, and board development.

Automating as many processes as possible and employing exceptional people gives me time to stay up to date on tax laws and changes. I had time to start a blog. I had time to start teaching with the Institute for Charitable Giving. I had time to start looking for speaking opportunities. In speaking,

I'm able to share my knowledge and my enthusiasm for what I do. I have a peculiar background for a nonprofit consultant, and it enables me to bridge the gap between wealth management and philanthropy. I can simplify complex concepts for audiences and draw them back to the basics, giving them confidence in their abilities and empowering them to act.

They say that if you love what you do, you'll never work a day in your life. I 100 percent call BS on that. Everyone who has ever navigated the road to success has risked something and worked tirelessly in pursuit of their dreams. The driving force behind reaching your desired destination is your commitment to excellence in everything you do. The true work is to never stop pushing and to never stop learning. It doesn't mean you're dissatisfied, and it certainly doesn't mean you cannot commit.

As I mentioned at the beginning of this book, if you look at my resume, you will think I either can't stick to anything or that I fail a lot and, consequently, start over a lot. "You'll never be happy," I've heard. "You'll never be satisfied. It will never be enough for you." But as I said from the start, the opposite is actually true.

I'm one of the happiest people I know. I'm satisfied with every aspect of my life, most of the time. You can accept where you are, be grateful for what you've accomplished, and still say, "What more can I do?" And if you're asking that, the next question is, "Can I do it on the bus that I'm currently on?"

Will the passengers on your bus naturally guide you to your desired destination? Will you have the courage to say, "These aren't the right passengers, but this is the right bus," and make the difficult decision to let some people off, or to say, "These passengers are great, but this bus isn't headed where I want to go," and pull the cord?

Being escorted off the bus is difficult. It's a blow to our ego and puts us on the side of the street, unsure of what will come next. Escorting people off the bus is incrementally more difficult. Whether you're firing people as employees or as friends, recognizing that your success is tied to being surrounded by the right people is half the battle. More challenging is escorting yourself off the bus. We get comfortable in our relationships (even when they are toxic), our lifestyle (even when we crave something different), and a reliable income (even when we want to earn more).

It is the comfort we crave. We accept less than what we want out of fear of discomfort and failure. But the world is full of buses and bus companies, and you are free to move about the cabin or signal to the driver you want to get off. As for failure, I refer to Dr. Pfau's Principle number fourteen: Unless you try to do something beyond what you have already mastered, you will never grow.

Trying something beyond what you have already mastered requires you to make bold changes. "Success" means something different to everyone. I succeed when I help someone achieve a goal they never imagined to be within reach. For the foster children entrusted to my care, it is finding them forever homes full of love and support. For my clients, it is watching them grow and expand their fundraising year after year so they can transform even more lives in their communities. For my partners, it is giving them the confidence to stretch beyond their initial view of possibilities. It is my willingness to accept and embrace change that empowers me to serve and lead.

As you reflect on where you are today and the success you aspire to tomorrow, are you surrounded by the right passengers? Are you on the right bus?

Lessons Learned:

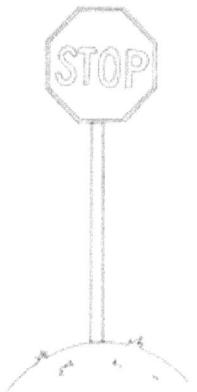

1. *"When we self-sabotage, it is often because we have a negative association between achieving the goal we aspire to and being the kind of person who has or does that thing."*

2. *Unless you try to do something beyond what you have already mastered, you will never grow.*

3. *Are you on the right bus?*

Afterward

Never underestimate the power of words. If you've made it to the end of this book, you've read a lot of stories about people who have impacted my life and given me the courage to dramatically change my trajectory. Time and again, people have encouraged me to examine the bus I was on, opened my eyes to other buses and bus lines that exist, empowered me to make transfers and changes, and believed in me when I had yet to believe in myself.

No one in the story of my life was under any obligation to share any of those words with me. They always say, "if you don't have anything nice to say, don't say anything at all." Where would I be today if people had held their tongues, simply because what they wanted to share with me wasn't what one might think of as "nice?" People who are willing to tell you difficult things from a place of love or growth arguably care about you more than anyone else.

I think about the words Melissa shared with me in my first job. They were tough. I think about what Mr. Brems said to me in the 8th grade. That was tough. Words that challenge you can push you to self-examine, take risks, and make positive changes. Having the courage to share a difficult message with someone with the right intention can be transformative. Borrowing confidence from someone you know who is cheering you on is only the first step. As your faith in your ability to keep building on what you have already mastered grows, so too the world in which you find inspiration expands. Whether through books, TedTalks, or formal education, never stop gaining confidence or getting some gumption from someone you admire.

To answer an earlier question, "What do you do if your parents are encouraging you to pursue something that offers stability, rather than pursuing your passions and dreams," by now you can probably look around your life and see that it isn't just parents who encourage us down a safe or conventional path. Relationships live and are nourished outside of passions, dreams, and life aspirations. Be kind, be patient, but do not sacrifice who you are or who you can become to please someone else. As Hans Urs von Balthasar famously wrote, "What you are is God's gift to you, what you become is your gift to God."

People ask me all the time, "How do you do all the things you do? Where do you find the time?" Not having children living at home frees up A LOT of time, but has not made my hands idle. For the last three years, I've been running two small businesses as the Executive Director of RaiseUp Families in Houston, Texas, and the President/CEO of Broad Oaks Consulting. I volunteer as a court-appointed Guardian ad Litem. I volunteer in a prison ministry. I read 30 books a year. I spend a lot of time with friends and family. I get a minimum of 45 minutes of intentional exercise each day. I meal prep. I love watching TV. I sleep 7-9 hours a day.

Here's the thing. Life has a way of expanding. Ask anyone who's ever had a child or anyone who has four children and is a high school Vice Principal, like my childhood friend, Alissa! Your life has a way of expanding for what's important to you. You don't have to choose between working, parenting, and making a difference in a stranger's life or in your community. You don't have to wait for one to finish before you start another. You can do it all. I promise you. Life will expand for you. The emphasis you place in each area of importance will vary depending on your season in life, however. Acknowledge that and embrace where you are today.

My own road to success has become less about me and more about developing and using the gifts God granted me to shine His light on Earth. He blessed me abundantly, and therefore I am not limited to one career, or even one career at a time. My range may be slightly wider than others, but in all of us lies the power to find success and fulfillment through courageous change.

The road to success is not easy and we all get tired. Whenever I start to feel defeated or lose my resolve, I return to the below quote by Marianne Williamson, and my flame reignites:

"Our deepest fear is not that we are inadequate. Our deepest fear is that we are powerful beyond measure. It is our light, not our darkness, that frightens us the most. We ask ourselves, 'Who am I to be brilliant, gorgeous, talented, fabulous?' Actually, who are you not to be? You are a child of God. Your playing small does not serve the world. There is nothing enlightened about shrinking so that other people won't feel insecure around you. We are all meant to shine, as children do. We were born to manifest the glory of God that is within us. It's not just in some of us; it's in everyone. And as we let our own light shine, we unconsciously give other people permission to do the same. As we are liberated from our own fear, our presence automatically liberates others."

After having read this book, how can you shine your light more brightly? Maybe it's as simple as offering a compliment to, or sharing a smile with, one stranger each day. Perhaps you make a greater effort to help your friends celebrate their big wins. You might download the "Purposeful Work Self-Assessment" available online at https://purposefulworkassessment.com or at this QR code and begin evaluating if your life and work exemplify your skills and abilities. Simply by purchasing this book, you have already put the wheels of change in motion as 10% of every book sold is donated to a nonprofit making a difference in the world.

If you are a nonprofit leader or sit on the board of directors of a nonprofit that has yet to reach its full potential, you can schedule a consultation to see if Broad Oaks Consulting is the right guide for your organization to future growth. If you work with a wealth management firm, trust company, or nonprofit seeking an eloquent speaker who will motivate your audience to action at your next meeting or event, you can submit an inquiry or schedule a consultation by scanning this QR Code below to start a conversation.

Thank you for taking this journey with me. I am incredibly grateful to everyone who reads this book and shares it with others. May you be inspired to navigate change more smoothly on your own road to success!

Works Cited in this Book

In case you're interested in reading any of the books mentioned that offered me inspiration, here's a quick list:

Good to Great, Jim Collins

Dark Horse, Todd Rose & Ogi Ogas

Atomic Habits, James Clear

The Da Vinci Code, Dan Brown

The Richest Man in Babylon, George Samuel Clason

Think and Grow Rich, Napoleon Hill

The Secret, Rhonda Byrne

Hope for the Flowers, Trina Paulus

The Four Winds by Kristin Hannah

The Unspoken Rules: Secrets to Starting Your Career Off Right, Gorick Ng

The Long Game, Dorie Clark

Greenlights, Matthew McConaughey

Just Mercy, A Story of Justice and Redemption, Bryan Stevenson

The Mountain is You, Brianna Wiest

THANK YOU FOR READING MY BOOK!

SCHEDULE YOUR CONSULTATION

If you're a nonprofit leader looking to partner with someone who has a long track record of growing sustainable businesses in both the for profit and nonprofit sectors, or an organization or company looking for a keynote speaker at your next event who will inspire and motivate your audience to action, schedule a consultation with Broad Oaks Consulting!

Scan the Code:

I appreciate your interest in my book, and value your feedback as it helps me improve future versions. I would appreciate it if you could leave your invaluable review on Amazon.com with your feedback. Thank you!

www.ingramcontent.com/pod-product-compliance
Lightning Source LLC
LaVergne TN
LVHW041332080426
835512LV00006B/419